I wish I'd had this book forty-five y[...]
going on in the world and the church now. *Brave Cities* is the manifestation of
seeking and listening. There are nuggets of truth in this book that on just their
singular level would change everything.
DR. JOHN M. PERKINS, civil rights activist; pastor; cofounder, Christian Community
Development Association (CCDA); author, *One Blood: Parting Words to the Church on
Race*

Brave Cities is a masterpiece. In this book, Hugh and Taylor present a rare and
compelling vision of "the kingdom come" in the various cities and localities
we inhabit. It is as brilliantly written as it is timely. A must-read.
ALAN HIRSCH, author of numerous books on missional church, leadership, and
spirituality; cofounder, Movement Leaders Collective and Forge Missional Training
Network

Halter and McCall have created a masterpiece. If you have concerns, as I do,
about the future of the Western church, read this. This book is equal parts
conviction and inspiration. It's not every day that authors can tell the truth and
leave you wanting more, and this book did just that. Far from the comfy couches
of theology, Taylor and Hugh have their sleeves rolled up and are living the future
now, with dirt under their nails and a twinkle in their eyes. These pilgrims invite
us to follow the One back into uncharted and wholehearted living—a return to
the start, remembering our first Love and warming our hearts back to life.
DANIELLE STRICKLAND, founder, Boundless Communications Inc.

As I read Hugh and Taylor's stories, their prophetic framework helped me see
what is simultaneously already here but also still on its way. It's not just our
models that need to change; it's our motifs and motivations. When you read
this book, you'll find yourself feeling caught up in the spirit of Hebrews 11:16,
longing and hoping for brave new cities.
DANIEL YANG, national director, Churches of Welcome at World Relief

Upon finishing *Brave Cities*, I have a profound sense of the significance and
gravitas of this book, one that I haven't felt since the one-two punch of Hirsch's
The Forgotten Ways and Halter and Smay's *The Tangible Kingdom* back in the
2000s. This book that Hugh and Taylor have given us is prophetically timed
for this moment. Like a slow-release pill, I am sure it will profoundly influence
a growing grassroots movement of the church that is hidden underneath the
surface here in America. This book will be considered one of the top five books
that shaped the next historic move of God that is rising and has already begun.
ROB WEGNER, Kansas City Underground, Shawnee Hub; regional director,
NewThing North America; coauthor, *The Starfish and the Spirit*

In *Brave Cities*, Hugh Halter and Taylor McCall brilliantly diagnose the problem at the heart of the declining church in the West. The solution they offer is a radical call to Christ-followers to meet people in the midst of their experiences and where they live. *Brave Cities* is a theologically grounded book written by practitioners for practitioners and is the wake-up call the church needs today.

DAVE FERGUSON, author, *B.L.E.S.S.: 5 Everyday Ways To Love Your Neighbor and Change the World*

Read Hugh Halter and Taylor McCall and learn the ways of a kingdom ecosystem. Escape the formulas of encrusted Christendom. Discover the church that exists among us wherever we live, whatever work we do, and whoever we share tables with. *Brave Cities* is like a muse calling out the best of us to be Christ's living church amidst a decaying world. Read each story and be caught up in Christ's kingdom, on earth as it is in heaven. My heartfelt recommendation.

DAVID FITCH, Lindner Chair of Evangelical Theology, Northern Seminary; author, *Faithful Presence*

This is not a manual for how to do church a bit differently; it is a blueprint for a revolutionary way to think about the church's place in society. McCall and Halter share an inspiring vision for how we can impact our cities by integrating benevolent businesses, justice works, and intentional households in order to help people find a whole new, full-hearted way to follow Jesus.

MICHAEL FROST, Morling College, Sydney

While I believe Jesus is present wherever his people are, he is always leading us to the edge of things. For years I have seen Hugh and Taylor explore and experiment on that innovative edge, where Jesus can be seen and heard most clearly. I am so thankful for this book and their leadership to all of us, to look for Jesus again on the missionary fringe.

BRIAN SANDERS, cofounder, Underground Network Tampa; author, *Microchurches*

All around the world, God has been moving his people into a new kind of life together. In this seminal book, Halter and McCall take us all into a fuller understanding of how we can live and work together to bring the light of God's kingdom into this dark world. They have blazed the trail for us to follow.

NEIL COLE, author, *Journeys, Primal Fire*, and *Organic Church*

You will need a roll of duct tape to go with this book because you will wear it out as a field guide on your mission of loving your city. Taylor and Hugh are not mere scribes and professors. They are sages and practitioners who have given us a practical and reproducible set of principles, along with stories that will both inspire your faith and unfurl your imagination along the journey.
LANCE FORD, author, *The Atlas Factor*

The biggest challenge for the Western church is to move from being church-centric to kingdom-centric. Hugh and Taylor's *Brave Cities* shows us what this looks like in real life. Their approach provides an off-ramp from irrelevant religious practice and an on-ramp for getting in on what God is up to.
REGGIE MCNEAL, senior fellow, Leadership Network; author, *Missional Renaissance* and *The Present Future*

There is a revolution coming, one that will change how the kingdom engages cities. In *Brave Cities*, McCall and Halter not only architect a vision years before its time, but they also unpack a playbook for how every city can become a brave city … if you've got the guts.
PEYTON JONES, author, *Church Plantology: The Art and Science of Planting Churches*; founder, NewBreed Training

Pick up the Etch A sketch of what you think you know about church and shake it. Then grab this book, sit on the ground, and see what God might inspire you to cultivate in the soil of your own brave city.
JESSIE CRUICKSHANK, author, *Ordinary Discipleship: How God Wires Us for the Adventure of Transformation;* coauthor, *Activating 5Q: A User's Guide*

In an age where deconstructing the church is like pickleball (it's easy and everyone's trying it), Hugh and Taylor have bravely and generously shared their journey in the harder task of reconstructing a viable alternative paradigm to "church as we've known it"—something beautiful, inspiring, holistic, and good.
LUCAS PULLEY, executive director, Underground Network

There's no question that Taylor and Hugh are on to something … and *Brave Cities* makes it enchantingly easy to grasp. Through biblical, practical, and, at times, hilarious reflection, they chart a disruptive course for those wanting the church to impact every aspect of life, not merely sustain what already exists. Whether as an individual considering the why, how, and what of your own missional alignment or as a vocational leader considering informed experimentation in church planting or a contemporary expression of kingdom community, *Brave Cities* will rightly inspire, challenge, and persuade your journey.

DR. MARK DEYMAZ, founder and directional leader, Mosaic Church of Central Arkansas and Mosaix Global Network; author, *Disruption* and *The Coming Revolution in Church Economics*

Brave Cities is like a good friend who says, "Hey, let's not give up on this church thing just yet. Let's talk a little more." If you can't quite give up on the beauty of the way of Jesus, the vision of the kingdom of God, and the possibilities of the community of saints and sinners called the church, then *Brave Cities* might be the gentle, practical, and provocative conversation partner you've been looking for. You'll be nudged toward wildness and freedom, toward being your true self, and toward an everyday reliance on Jesus for your next steps of courageous adventure.

KEVIN COLÓN, church planter and pastor; government communications professional

No one who is engaged in the way of Jesus can deny that there has been a shift in the common understanding of church. Hugh and Taylor are fully committed to walking you through this rethinking in this comprehensive work. As I read, I cheered for a lot of it. I wrestled against some of it. But I am grateful for all of it. I've been in plenty of spaces with these guys, and they're the real deal. Read this book. Use it to challenge and shake you, and to press in to where you disagree and see where you come out of that process. And let *Brave Cities* encourage you that the kingdom of Jesus is always advancing, and his church is alive and well and strong.

JASON SHEPPERD, Church Project Network and Good City

My husband and I have lived and worked in impoverished inner-city areas over the years and know only too well the challenges involved. Several years ago, we had the privilege of visiting Taylor and Lindsey McCall and seeing their pioneering work in Birmingham, Alabama. To say we were impressed would be an understatement. They, and the folks in their community, were transforming their very run-down segment of the city and the lives of those who lived there. *Brave Cities* discusses the principles behind this kind of movement with colorful examples throughout. I give it my highest recommendation!

FELICITY DALE, author, *An Army of Ordinary People* and *The Rabbit and the Elephant*

BRAVE CITIES

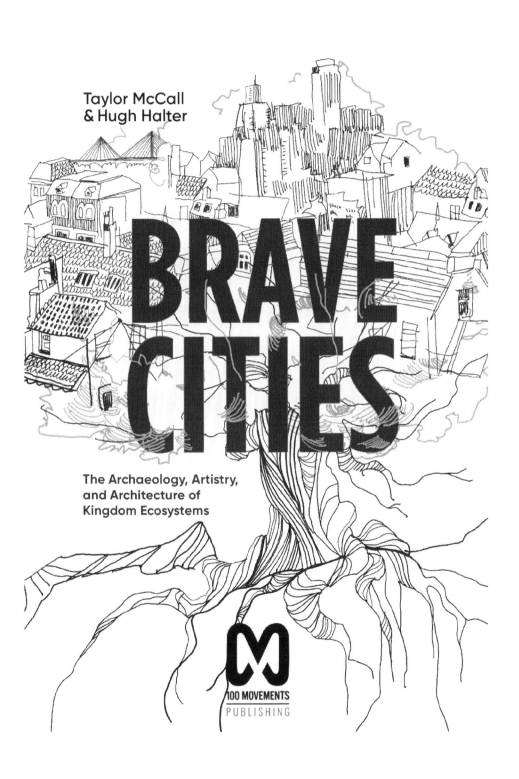

Taylor McCall
& Hugh Halter

BRAVE CITIES

The Archaeology, Artistry,
and Architecture of
Kingdom Ecosystems

100 MOVEMENTS
PUBLISHING

First published in 2024 by 100 Movements Publishing
www.100mpublishing.com
Copyright © 2024 by Taylor McCall and Hugh Halter

Library of Congress Control Number: 2023923045

ISBN 978-1-955142-51-9 (print)
ISBN 978-1-955142-52-6 (eBook)

Cover and interior design: Anastasia Yaroshchuk

Editorial team: Joel Varner, Carolyn Smith, and Mercedes Thomas

100 Movements Publishing
An imprint of Movement Leaders Collective
Richmond, Virginia
www.movementleaderscollective.com

We would like to dedicate this book to the brave practitioners. First, we think of our families who have lived this story with us; and second, we think of the inspirational people we have met along the way who quietly and humbly pursue something that is at least a shadow of the beauty of the kingdom. We see you and are writing this so that others will find hope and faith in your stories.

CONTENTS

PROLOGUE

The Day Everything Changed in Surfing and the Church

That which we obtain too cheaply we esteem too lightly.
THOMAS PAYNE

Does not a builder count the cost before starting to build?
JESUS

In March of 2020, 99 percent of US churches stopped gathering. Sure, fewer and fewer folks were already coming to worship services, but we still had enough people around to justify sticking to the status quo. We held tight to our programs and our preaching, and ignored the church's complicity with consumerism, racism, classism, and sexism. But when COVID-19 hit, both pastors and parishioners were forced to take a break from the relentless demands and busyness of religion, and instead spent their time and money on DIY home projects, Pelotons, Sprinter vans, and even surfboards. What was supposed to be a fifteen-day quarantine to "stop the spread" turned into months, and in some places, years. But when the quarantines finally lifted, more than one million people never came back to church … and the church world drastically changed.[1]

Although the impact of the pandemic on the church is probably not news to you, what you may not be aware of is the impact the pandemic had on the world of surfing. According to most people in the surf community, COVID-19 radically affected what was already a frustrated community, due to the sudden influx of people with brand-new surfboards and no experience.

One of the sacred places I (Hugh) love to go at least once a year is a spot called Pleasure Point in Santa Cruz, California. I stay with my buddy Mark at his home nestled on a rocky bluff that is the furthest west-pointing spot jutting out into Monterey Bay in the Pacific Ocean. Early one morning five years ago, we sat around a fire with about eight young men—some of whom were world-class surfers—fifty feet from crashing waves that broke just beneath the rock ledge holding Mark's home. While eating handcrafted oats with sautéed apples and cinnamon, we talked about life, women, Jesus, and the state of surfing. That day, Mark graciously invited me to cross off a lifetime item on my bucket list: riding a real wave. He sanctioned me and my "blue board" to go out into the water. Blue boards are what every entry-level surfer gets when they rent their board from a shop just off the beach. It signals to the other surfers that these are the people about to destroy your beautiful day of surfing! Learning to ride my first wave was one of the most physically exhausting and exhilarating moments of my life. Since that first time in the water five years ago, I've returned to Pleasure Point many times. However, I don't go back in the water—even though Mark invites me. I'd rather sit, drink a coffee, and watch the local scene unfold. I prefer spectating because of what I've learned about the culture.

The surf culture in Santa Cruz is unique, and many books and movies have chronicled that way of life. Today, many call surfing a "sport," but if you said that back in the day (or even now, to some extent) the real "core" surf community would either laugh at you or punch you in the face. For them, surfing has always been a way of life—with its own customs, unwritten codes, and unique cultural and contextual nuances. But in many parts of the world, maintaining this surf culture has become something of a fight for survival.

Many in the surfing world are asking, "What killed surf culture?"

Was it the advent of the wetsuit, which allowed people to stay in the water way too long? Perhaps it was the surf cam that unveiled every secret surf spot, causing overcrowding and allowing unskilled surfers into world-class waves. Was it the internet, with its surf forecasts, which revealed to everyone the best hours to catch waves? Or maybe it was the advent of the Wavestorm—that hundred-dollar, blue Costco surfboard—that equipped everyone to dabble in surfing with no real financial sacrifice. Or the surf schools, treating the oceans like a schoolyard, pushing people by the thousands into the surf break in front of all the other surfers because they only have an hour to get these people up, or their Yelp review is going to suck. Or does it go all the way back to the 1959 movie *Gidget* that made surfing and surfers cool and started what we now know as the "surfing industry"?[2] If calling surfing a sport gets the die-hards' water boiling, consider how they feel about becoming an "industry." But that industry now caters to the Silicon Valley consumers who have bought up all the real estate, leaving the core or real surfing community to live out of their '72 Volkswagen buses or single-wide mobile trailers—waking up with pizza on their dashboard and sand in their ass instead of looking at the shore from their $5 million bungalows.

Once upon a time, the only way you could get to some of the great surfing spots was by scaling down twenty-foot cliffs. But now, beautiful cement stairs make it easy for anyone to access the best waves. The OG surfers were anti-industry because, as we all know, industries do what's best for the industry, not what's best for the people already involved. Jesus said it this way, "For wide is the gate and broad is the road that leads to destruction, and many enter through it. But small is the gate and narrow the road that leads to life, and only a few find it" (Matthew 7:13–14). So now, what was once a narrow way is dying a wide, slow death.

See, surfing, like being a part of a Jesus movement (his church), was always a lifestyle, a way of life. You could be it to your core. In fact, to survive, you had to. You had to know someone who could teach you. You had to be mentored into "wave riding." You had to meet with board shapers, then patiently wait for them to customize your board—or better, be taught how to shape your own. You couldn't just walk into Costco and put your blue board on top of your pallet of toilet paper. You were all in or you didn't go in. You could stand off at a distance out of respect, as I did, or you could join in, but you couldn't just try it recreationally. You went without surf forecasts and just navigated whatever the conditions were. And life was good.

Back to the question, "What killed surfing?" Although the pandemic had a huge impact, no one blames COVID-19. Nor should we blame the church's struggle on this unique span of two years. Consumerism was already destroying both groups. The pandemic did add to the misery, but it mostly exposed the sicknesses related to making narrow things wide.

And so the surf community has started their own reformation. The hope is that the purists—the all-in lifestyle camp—will emerge once again as the true north of surfing. Yes, there will always be blue-boarders, and the core community isn't even trying to get them out of the water; but what the core has resolved is that they will never be co-opted or consumer-driven. They'll just surf with the ones they've been surfing with forever—the small groups of friends who want the full life; who want to be courageous, cold, scared, challenged, and to harness the ocean, catch a bulge of energy that has traveled thousands of miles in the form of a wave, and ride it ... for nothing more than the fun and the intrinsic meaning of the experience.

We wonder if the church can reform like this as well.

What would happen if the church world looked inside itself and asked why one million people decided not to return after COVID-19? (And that's just a fraction of the forty million people who have left since the '70s.[3]) Could it be that the pandemic just exposed the recreational, corporate, consumer culture that was already there? Did our adventuresome family on a mission become a business or even an industry? Did our focus on getting as many blue-boarders as possible into the water do what inevitably happens to anything truly good and pure? Could it be that the church now has an opportunity to reflect on why people are abandoning consumer Christianity? Could we reclaim "core" Jesus culture?

Whenever I'm with Mark, he sees me on the shore watching him surf. Yes, he knows I get it now and that I don't want to reenter the waves without a serious commitment; but, for some reason, he keeps inviting me in. Apparently, it used to be that ten-year-olds would have to "cut kelp" with a knife for a year before locals would let them into the surf lineup. Like Mark, Jesus keeps calling us to surf—and he's already cut the kelp for us. We don't have to pay all our dues again, but we would be wise not to make light of that opportunity ... or go in recreationally again. We must care about the legacy and lifestyle of following Jesus and being the church. We don't have to be good at surfing or pick it up quickly, but we do need to honor the story enough to give it our best shot. We really do.

This book is for men and women who are tired of watching on the sidelines. And they're also tired of being a part of the blue-board culture that has made a stench of consumer religion out of what was meant to be an aroma of Christ. This book is like Mark, who continues to include me in the community. Standing on the cliff, just watching because you see the blue-boarders wrecking the thing, isn't an excuse anymore. Truth is, no one knows what's next or what will become of the church as we know it, but chances are, what's next won't be the answer. All we know is Jesus is inviting his church to surf.

I once asked Mark what his best day surfing was. He answered without hesitation. It was in Tel Aviv in knee-high waves with his wife and world-champion surfer CJ Nelson, playing in the beach break like seven-year-olds, rolling with the waves, giggling like children—no rankings, no lineup, no drop-in, no sponsorship, no audience, no commercialism ... just waves and friends. By far the best day.

The best days of the church are ahead of us. But who will get to ride the waves? The committed, the all-in crew, the core, the lifestyle gang, the saints, the ambassadors, the ministers of reconciliation, the priests of this new nation, and the family we call the church.

If you choose to take your first steps toward the waves and continue with us in this book of observations, we promise you a few things: We won't BS you; and we won't give you keys, best practices, or assurances that you'll return home safely at the end of each day. But we hope that we will rekindle in you a desire to be part of the all-in crew for the King and his kingdom. And, we will give you a clear call to dig like archaeologists, to create like artists, and to architect simple tables where people can detect the aroma of the King and his kingdom.

We look forward to hearing the stories of your brave cities,

Taylor and Hugh

"

COULD IT BE THAT THE CHURCH NOW HAS AN
OPPORTUNITY TO REFLECT ON WHY PEOPLE ARE
ABANDONING CONSUMER CHRISTIANITY? COULD
WE RECLAIM "CORE" JESUS CULTURE?

"

Act One

MUSIC NOT MATH

Embracing the Avant-Garde Church

*Sing a new song to the L*ORD*! Let the whole
earth sing to the L*ORD*!*
PSALM 96:1 NLT

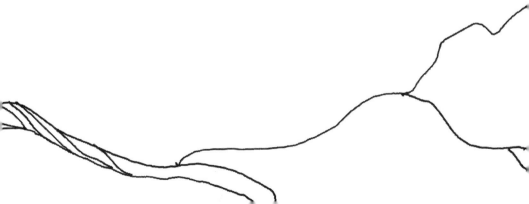

A few months back, Hugh came to me (Taylor) and told me he had decided to be a country music songwriter. Apparently, on a flight somewhere, he was inspired by the simplicity of a Kenny Chesney song and thought that since he's written ten or so books, he could write at least one country song and hit the jackpot. I told Hugh if he put pen to paper, I'd be able to put some music to it. So a week later, he emailed me the lyrics to "On the Fence Line." It wasn't half bad, so I spent a couple of days tweaking the lyrics and composing the music. A few weeks later, I recorded the song in a friend's studio. Everyone seemed to love it ... except Hugh. As we discussed our stylistic goals for this song, it was clear we were not coming at it with the same intentions. Hugh had two goals. First, he wanted to finally "get paid," as he called it. The poor guy has been hustling and giving his time and life away pro bono for forty years, and I couldn't fault his desire to go pro. Second, he had a dream of taking his wife, Cheryl, and me and my wife, Lindsey, to the Grammys. Now I would love for Hugh to accomplish these two goals because I'd benefit too. However, Hugh was understanding when I told him that I did not share, nor could I ever share, his aspirations. You see, I'm cursed with artistic passions. I took that song and tried to put honesty to it, regardless of any payout. I wish I could break this rule, but I've never been able to see or pursue an artistic venture with dollar signs on it.

I believe music has to be art, fully and purely. We so easily turn music into math, as if we think there's a formula to great music ... and for chart toppers there probably is. But for music to be truly artistic by nature, it can't be a simple formula.

Now consider the kingdom of God or the church. Meditate for a minute or ten on how much creativity God put into these two beautiful ideas. This last year, we took a group of men on a twelve-month journey through the book of Acts. We didn't plan on taking an entire year, but each story was like a full-length Netflix series. Each "act" was full of nuance and contextual curveballs. God's church had *no* prescription or apparent formula. Some days nothing happened. On other days, thousands turned to God. Some days ended in a jail sentence or a shipwreck and others in a powerful moment of healing. When Jesus taught about the kingdom and how it functioned, he likened it to a mustard seed, a dragnet, a pearl, or a piece of land that someone would sell everything to buy (see Matthew 13). When God was building his prototype of the church, there wasn't a Bible. There wasn't a church-planter toolkit or a downloadable book on the subject. The church consisted of a new family, a new citizenship, a new priesthood, and a new messianic community that was learning how to reach into the uttermost parts of the earth. At that time, no one knew what problems or possibilities lay in inviting one's next-door neighbor into this new community, let alone people at the ends of the earth. So it is in our day.

Now, in the year 2024, few of the older paradigms or equations are working for those inside or outside the church. Therefore, as followers of Jesus, we must be people of music. We cannot use the Bible as a math book containing axioms to memorize and formulas to spout. It was never meant to be wielded like a gun or sledge-hammer or a manual you pull out of the glove compartment with a schematic for global domination. The Bible must return to its purpose as a collection of love letters from God and a few of his original musicians who lived as aliens and sojourners in a home that wasn't theirs. We then listen to the music of God and those original musicians and learn how to "sing a new song" that reveals God's kingdom to the world in a way that makes sense in our time and place (Psalm 96:1).

Being from Alton, Illinois, we boast that the acclaimed jazz musician Miles Davis hails from our humble town. Apparently, Davis was told if he wanted to hone his natural raw talent, he should do it at The Juilliard School—the most prestigious academy for young artists. Davis went to Juilliard, but he dropped out because he wanted to perform full-time; and when he left, he ran into a man named Charlie Parker who simply invited Davis to play his trumpet with a fellow artist and pick up a few ideas. No manual, no schedule, no expectations, no tests. It was in this environment that Davis learned the heart of jazz—a style of music that is all about improvisation, soul, and feel.

It seems the church could do with learning a few lessons from Charlie Parker and Miles Davis. Why do we miss this creative framework and keep relying on an institutional structure? Why do we keep putting our hope in seminary-trained clinicians? Why do we call preparation for ministry "homiletics," "hermeneutics," "theology," and "end-times study"? Why do we ask future leaders to complete two- to six-year internships on hospital calls, the performance of weddings and funerals, and administration of ordinances and sacraments? And why do we pay the clerics (the pastors/teachers) to produce sermon-centric services instead of funding the artists (the apostolic ones) to experiment with anything new? There are, of course, many reasons institutional forms of anything resist creative nuance. The fear of something new, concern for investing and supporting something that may not work, letting go of personal gain, the flat-out disregard for the missional essence and call of "the church," and so many other reasons often prevent progress, change, and creativity.

What if we could simply find the young Miles Davises and connect them with the older Charlie Parkers of the world, and ultimately hook them up with the Master jazz musician himself? We wonder if we might get some new expressions of church.

This movement we're invited into was always meant to be more like an underground jazz joint or a speakeasy.[1] How many times did Jesus say, "Don't tell anyone" or "Now's not the time"? Or what about when his popularity was booming, and the crowds thronged around him, and he told everyone to "eat his flesh and drink his blood" (John 6:53–59), knowing full well it would disorient and offend almost everyone following him at the time? It wasn't that he wanted us to be ashamed or to keep quiet for quiet's sake. It wasn't that he wanted us to purposely run people off. But he knew that pop faith wasn't going to change the world.

When asked why jazz wasn't part of the pop scene, Herbie Hancock purportedly said in *Prose Magazine*,

> People don't care about the music itself anymore, but about who makes the music. The public is more interested in celebrities and how a certain artist is famous than music. ... [They no longer have] a transcendental connection to music and its quality. Just want the glamour. Jazz doesn't want to be part of it. Do you know why? It's not about humility, or arrogance, a posture, "we don't want to be famous, we're underground." None of that. Jazz is about the human soul, not about the appearance. Jazz has values, teaches to live the moment, work together, and especially to respect the next. When musicians gather to play together, you have to respect and understand what the other does. Jazz in particular is an international language that represents freedom, because of its roots in slavery. Jazz makes people feel good about themselves.[2]

The movement of Jesus' church, like jazz, isn't about fame or popularity. It's about coming together with other musicians to create new music that lifts others up.

MAKING ART

Both of us have gotten to be on the front edges of many new church conversations. We've been invited to shark-tank events where would-be kingdom investors listen to pitches for new iterations of church. We've been at secret apostolic round tables with the who's who of contemporary missiologists and theologians. We speak at the conferences that often define the conversation the wider church will have in the coming year. And we've been fortunate to be associated with some of the most prolific thought-leaders and practitioners of our time. We've seen in our ecclesial journey the mega-multi-site emphasis born of the church-growth movement. We've seen the early organic shift (thanks, Neil Cole) that preceded the contemporary missional movement of the last two decades. We've seen a focus on missional communities, microchurch, and every form of disciple-making processes and organizations. All were helpful in their time to some degree, and all had a sharp edge.

Although we count it an honor to be in these conversations—and we love and respect anyone who cares enough about Christ's bride to look at her in the mirror—we must raise our hands now and ask, "Why are we still trying to fix or formula the church?" Maybe the problem is that, no matter what the focus is, art can never come from a formula. It's impossible to look at one leader's legacy and try to copy it. Sure, it can be picked apart and turned into a paint-by-number, but instead of being creative art, it will be more of a dumbed-down, smudgy attempt at effecting a quick fix on something that can't be fixed quickly.

We think this is why, in Matthew 13, Jesus doesn't mince words with those who are desperately looking for easy answers. "Why do you speak in parables?" they ask. They obviously were frustrated, just like we are when Jesus doesn't make things crystal clear. And why doesn't he? I mean, doesn't he want us to get after it and nail it?

His response:

> "Because the knowledge of the secrets of the kingdom of heaven has been given to you, but not to them. Whoever has will be given more, and they will have an abundance. Whoever does not have, even what they have will be taken from them. This is why I speak to them in parables: 'Though seeing, they do not see; though hearing, they do not hear or understand.'"
>
> MATTHEW 13:11–13

Hmm. This should make us all laugh in exuberant joy or shudder in an anxious rage. Jesus is speaking in parables because people want him to provide the paint-by-number version of the Sistine Chapel by Michelangelo. And he's saying it won't happen. But for those who dare to create, listen, beg, and dig for treasure, aah, he's going to reveal the colors, angles, depth, and texture of his emerging art.

To the pastor (in the most classic sense of the word), we know you want to help everyone. We understand the desire and the pure heart behind wanting to make the narrow way as broad as possible and to lower the branch of kingdom living so low that anyone can grab a piece of fruit. We know you think it's right to try to unify the church and give people baby steps forward, but we encourage you to move beyond these pursuits. We don't think Jesus wants you to make narrow ways wide. We don't think you can dig for other people. Jesus commanded everyone who wants to be his disciple to "deny themselves and take up their cross daily and follow" (Luke 9:23). We cannot carry people's crosses for them to make them disciples. And we certainly don't think it's a strategic use of your time to help everyone who "needs" you. You can deliver sermons, give time, and run all kinds of programs for people who will just trample those pearls under their worldly concerns and pressures—and what you'll end up with will just look like a pig trough (see Matthew 7:6).

We are calling you to consider the one life God is giving you and suggesting that the moment you begin your creative pathway is the moment you decide to live the narrow way, regardless of who follows, applauds, acknowledges, understands, or finances your new life.

So ... back to art.

To be truly art, a thing must be done for the passion of it, clean and simple. You may hit it big—as Hugh hoped to with his country song—but most won't, and history has proven it might not be in your best interests to do so. So you better be in it for the beauty of what God creates out of your sold-out life. No amount of money can buy it, and it can't be taken away. As Liam Neeson said in the 1995 movie *Rob Roy*, "Honor is a gift a man [or woman] gives himself."[3] From this point on, it's up to you to start digging for yourself.

This book is all about the art ... about the music ... and about following the bigger, wilder, more mysterious, more exciting way of Jesus. And we're going to help you put away the math book. We want to give you access to some other artists and musicians who might just decide to give you some of their sheet music. But we hope you'll always remember Miles Davis and Charlie Parker and dig for authentic relationships to push you to create instead of impersonate.

THE CHURCH AS AN AVANT-GARDE MOVEMENT

Consider the meaning of "avant-garde." The term refers to something new, unusual, or experimental, especially in the arts or the people introducing them. The adjective form would connote "favoring or introducing experimental or unusual ideas." Consider also the word "iconoclast," which means "image-destroyer" or "idol-breaker."

Now consider Jesus, his kingdom, and his church. Every word Jesus spoke and everything he did utterly broke molds, rules, laws, and formulas that people had created to put God and his kingdom in a box. And when the kingdom broke through in tangible ways, it created intangible moments that broke people's hearts. So God's church, God's people, and the way they live should also reflect something of the iconoclastic, avant-garde aspect of God's nature.

The kingdom is "breaking in," as we say, in moments, not formulas. When I (Hugh) was at my daughter's class at her studio, Commons Yoga, I noticed I couldn't make it through the session without being overcome with tears. It was embarrassing until I heard and realized that other people were having the same experience. No, it wasn't the pain of holding poses or doing awkward stretches. There was something about the way she led the class, her presence, the music she chose, and the people who needed this one hour to escape the struggle and trauma of life in a rough town. The power was in the moments, and you just can't script that.

Maybe you've heard about one of the best restaurants in the world that is now shut down. It was called El Bulli, in Spain's Costa Brava. Anthony Bourdain, in his award-winning show *No*

Reservations, chronicled the astonishing story of El Bulli's head chef, Ferran Adrià, as he hosted his final dinner.[4] Adrià was renowned for his innovations in the culinary arts, and for creating sixty-four-course meals that would last for four or five hours, and where each course was a bite of something no one had ever tasted before. He taught the power of food but also the power of sequence, timing, waiting, lingering, sharing, explaining what was being offered, pairing, appreciation, and thankfulness. While being filmed for *No Reservations*, Adrià shared every bite with Bourdain as if it was the first time he had savored it. Full-hearted, laughing, and joyful, Adrià was still amazed at how each bite tasted. He was not just creating; he enjoyed and experienced his own creation.

In most restaurants, staff rarely eat the food they prepare for others, but Adrià treated his staff differently, encouraging them to create and partake of a meal together before each evening's service. He believed that the two greatest things in life are to help people enjoy special moments and to give people something to think about. As you can imagine, the revolutionary culture he created at El Bulli spread to other restaurants around the world.

So why did he shut this perfectly successful, iconoclastic restaurant down? To break another mold. His desire was to spend the rest of his time creating an institute or school to apprentice the next generation of gastronomic agitators. He believed that the highest form of generosity is to share courage. Like the fifteenth-century Medici family, who funded and completely paid the tab for the Renaissance artists, Adrià also believed the best use of time is not just to create but to also foster, inspire, and equip creativity.

One chef who shared the table with Bourdain on Adrià's final night wept as he articulated how his life had been forever transformed by this one man's creativity. A young apprentice at the start of his culinary career, this chef used to be on the cooking line in a fast-paced restaurant. Speaking through tears, he said, "We came without a spirit, and we left with a soul."

This is the power of breaking away from oppressive rules and traditions; of moments of the kingdom that break through to our hearts.

A BRAVE CITY

We are using the term "brave city" to describe a kingdom ecosystem that breaks into the world in new and creative ways. It's a community of people intentionally held together and propelled forward by their collective calling to Jesus and his avant-garde artistic activity in the world to help people experience deep transformation. Let's call it a place of genuine good news, where coffee, reconciliation, discipleship, worship, enterprise, whiskey, fitness, homes, activism, justice, and community development (and any other element a seeker seeks) all become the ingredients of a true biblical community. At least that's our story in Alton. In other cities, the ingredients may be different.

We've scratched and sniffed the surface of several historical accounts, including the cities of refuge in Deuteronomy, the early church in Acts, the ark communities of Petra, as well as the Benedictines, the Trappists, the Moravians, and the Methodists. We've also explored more contemporary expressions such as the communities in Globe, Arizona; Church of the Savior in late-twentieth-century Washington, DC; and many unnamed ecosystems we are presently coaching and learning from. In each of these examples, something emerges about the church as a true justice movement, a family, and a marketplace network. That reality keeps us reaching forward for ourselves, our kids, and thousands of church leaders who are looking for something more.

These kingdom ecosystems are examples of God's people living out God's command to the exiled Israelites captive in Babylon: "Build homes, and plan to stay. Plant gardens, and eat the food they produce ... And work for the peace and prosperity of the city where I sent you into exile. Pray to the LORD for it, for its welfare will determine your welfare" (Jeremiah 29:5–7 NLT). Providing jobs, food, drink, and sustaining goods was essential in the call of the church in ancient times—and it still is. Our goal cannot be just to share good news. We must, as they did in the book of Acts, share financial resources, share hope for an improved neighborhood, share our fathers and mothers with those who have none, and see all of life as an integrated worship song offered up to God. The Benedictine motto that has guided our work in Alton is *ora et labora* (pray and work) which means that to pray is to work and the work is the prayer—dissolving the divide between sacred and secular, clergy and laity, spiritual formation and manual labor, and thus highlighting the Lord's divine presence in all things.

Consider our brave city in Alton, which has thirty missionaries and eleven microbusiness ventures connected to a central coffee/coworking space in the heart of a depressed, thirty-thousand-person town. We incubate "good works," including a donation-based yoga studio, a photography studio, a woodcraft studio, an eighty-acre equine therapy farm, a coffee-roasting company, a music studio, a brunch café, and many other new business startups. This house of "brands" has a centralized administration and finance team that serves the kingdom ecosystem instead of just providing a public worship gathering. We disciple leaders and the lost in a very low-key fashion, connecting monthly worship spaces, Tuesday leadership trainings, men's whiskey/theology gatherings, and house gatherings into an ecosystem that, according to city leaders and many locals, has changed the spirit and atmosphere of Alton. No, we don't think we are doing much at all, but after five years we are sensing some appreciation, and we feel like people would be sad to see us go if that were ever to happen.

Consider a brave city in the southern city of San Antonio, Texas. Now seven years old, they have a community events center, handcrafted-root-beer company, branding company, and serve a meal and hold a church gathering on the back patio of a local pizza joint. Students and churches around the city send their next-generation "missionaries in training" to their immersions.

Consider a brave city in Portland, Oregon that started out of a CrossFit gym. This group created a space of belonging for the under-thirties crowd, and half of their clients are from the queer community. Their leader both laments and laughs that the businesses they have started have had far more impact than their "church" gatherings; and they are expanding into a business incubator, a coaching and consulting business, and have just purchased a thirty-thousand-square-foot building so they can offer a much larger business and social space.

Consider a brave city in Tampa, Florida that has as its front door a bike shop in a shopping mall but whose focus is on men and women without homes. Another brave city that meets in the same mall connected with them and focuses on unique mission-based microchurches throughout the Tampa metroplex.

Consider a brave city in Phoenix, Arizona, that since starting five years ago has developed a coffee shop, hot-chicken joint, neighborhood dive bar, high-end hamburger restaurant, coffee roaster, comic-book design company, and holds weekly Sunday morning church gatherings as well as special spiritual formation retreats up in the mountains.

Consider a brave city in the richest suburb of Washington, DC that has purchased a ten-acre piece of prime real estate and has developed a school, music venue, events space, commissary kitchen to train local chefs, and is looking to build out a live-in missionary training house for young leaders. They have a worshiping community of about one hundred and serve the growing refugee community in what would otherwise be known as the "rich side of town."

Consider a brave city in Boise, Idaho that operates as the only church in its valley of 2,500 homes and that just took over the one central business development, serving coffee by day and spirits by night. As the only "church option," they are doggedly training house communities and asking people to pastor their own friends.

(We're not sharing individual's names or other specific information about any of these examples because most of them are pretty new to their story. We know the pressure it creates when people want to "check you out.")

In each of these cases, no one needs parishioners to pay the pastoral paychecks. The businesses cover livelihoods, and people come to faith and are discipled into the community, however they define it. They never talk about numbers or ministries or programs. They only talk about people and what they are hoping to keep building into their kingdom ecosystems. And they don't follow a formula. They experiment with expressing the kingdom of God in new and unusual ways, like avant-garde iconoclasts, often breaking with tradition to see God create something new.

YOU'RE FREE

In 2016, I (Hugh) was speaking at a conference called Verge, in Austin, Texas. It was the largest conference on the missional church in America. During one of my sessions, a stranger named Shawn came up to me and told me he had just come to faith in his early forties and asked me if I would consider coaching him. I was honored that my story and the way our family did mission caught his imagination, but I knew I couldn't really walk with him because he lived in another city. "Man, I wish I could," I told him. "But I know God will lead you." He asked me what he should do. All I said was, "Shawn, you're free … just go do whatever Jesus tells you."

And so he and his wife, Inga, did.

Shawn left his successful business, and he and Inga moved into the poorest area of the city—the little township of Portland, five minutes west of downtown Louisville, Kentucky. Just yesterday, Taylor and I visited their kingdom ecosystem called Love City, which began in 2017. We asked him how it started, and they said they just moved in, opened their home, and threw lavish parties for hookers, addicts, and pretty much anyone who didn't have a home or friends. Soon, hundreds of people knew them, and then the ecosystem began to grow. In short order, they took over a school building. Soon a community space, after-school program, athletic facility, K–8 grade school, barbeque joint, community gardens, and more emerged. Then they were given a huge one-hundred-year-old Catholic church, where they hold twice-monthly worship gatherings. Yes, they do have a worship gathering in the church building, but Shawn and Inga would be the first to say that church happens all the time, every day.

In fact, as we visited, we got to experience a monthly all-church gathering, full of beautifully connected white, brown, and Black folk. Shawn told them the story of how he and I met. He invited me to look around and see what God had done, simply because I reminded Shawn that he was free to go and just follow Jesus.

When you think of the church, never forget that it takes nothing but a willing vessel and the leading of the Spirit to create something small or big anywhere in the world. Shawn didn't know how to do any of this, but God provided, and it's one of the most impressive ecosystems we've seen in the US. As Jesus said, the Holy Spirit can and does guide us into all truth (John 16:13).

Bondage, pressure, costly programs, debt, and decline follow the consumer-Christian church. There's the consistent need to market, invite, appease, brand, and compete with the spirituality and performance of the next guy or gal. Bigger, better, bigger, better. But where Jesus is and where he leads always brings freedom from all of this! It is for freedom that Christ set you free (Galatians 5:1). Don't worry about others' perceptions of who you are or whether you are legitimate. Just start creating and acknowledge in faith that God is building, and will continue to build, his church.

When you're running free and fast and at the cadence of God's heartbeat, many obstacles are going to appear in your path and slow you down. Lindsey and I (Taylor) always tell our kids, the reason we don't want you to sin is because we want you to run fast. Don't let anything—not sin, and certainly not another person's judgment—slow you down. Remember, sin isn't simply bad things you do; it is also not doing the good things that God is asking you to do.

"If anyone, then, knows the good they ought to do and doesn't do it, it is sin for them" (James 4:17). As the writer of Hebrews warned, do not let anything or anyone bind you and slow you down in your faithful following of Jesus:

> Let us throw off everything that hinders and the sin that so easily entangles. And let us run with perseverance the race marked out for us, fixing our eyes on Jesus, the pioneer and perfecter of faith. … Consider him who endured such opposition from sinners, so that you will not grow weary and lose heart.
>
> HEBREWS 12:1–3

For many, "church" is still a place you go or attend. But we imagine a day when people will ask, "Who are you churching with?" or "How are you churching up in your town?" We hope that more and more people will one day say, "This whole ecosystem and everyone in it is church for me." In a statement like that, we can find freedom. And whenever we communicate this vision to people, although they don't entirely get what we're saying, they always nod as if it is something they want.

DAWNING OF A NEW DAY

As we conclude this cursory overview of kingdom ecosystems, we wanted to end with a story that encapsulates everything we've been saying. About four years ago, we were meeting with a leader in Ferguson, Missouri, which is just seven miles from Alton. This person had heard about Lantern Network, the marketplace mission we pioneered in Alton, and had come to see what we were up to a year prior. He was considering starting the only coffee shop in Ferguson and asked us to meet him at a yoga café on a cold January morning.

As you probably know, the infamy of Ferguson began on August 9, 2014, when eighteen-year-old African American Michael Brown was fatally shot by a white police officer. Riots erupted in the town, causing the nation to awaken from a long slumber of repressed racial injustice and ignorance of the social issues that have plagued our country. Many now refer to Ferguson as the birthplace of the modern justice movement in the US, though there is still much work to be done.

As we shared our common story and hope for the church, this young African-American leader shared his journey to Ferguson. Then he told the story of another man whose legacy he was looking to follow—a man named Josiah Henson, the inspiration for Uncle Tom in Harriet Beecher Stowe's 1852 novel *Uncle Tom's Cabin*.[5]

Henson was born into slavery in Port Tobacco, Maryland, in 1789. In 1830, he escaped to Ontario, Canada, and lived out his abolitionist beliefs in the community of Dawn, Ontario. Originally founded as a place of refuge for escaped slaves, this community established a vocational school to help former slaves develop marketable skills. The Dawn Settlement's purpose statement was to "'cultivate the entire being, and to elicit the fairest and fullest possible development of the physical, intellectual and moral powers,' and to provide Black Canadians with the skills they needed to prosper and to disapprove the racist beliefs."[6] Henson was building a comprehensive kingdom ecosystem so ex-slaves could live independently inside an interdependent community.

The Dawn Settlement grew as a school, trade institute, mill, brickyard, farm, and church. Their woodworking and furniture-making skills became known worldwide, as word spread from kings and queens to other dignitaries about their fine craftsmanship. At its height, the community cared for five hundred residents and inspired Stowe's groundbreaking novel.

Imagine just for a moment, if you can, living a life of slavery. Imagine every day is without hope, full of emotional and physical trauma. Imagine no palpable sense of self-worth, and every moment you work holds no hope of personal gain or sustaining financial benefit for your family. Imagine the utter sense of loss.

Then imagine you've endured months of brutal, fearful, hungry travel, and you wake up to find yourself being joyfully accepted by a new community of true friends who share their food and shelter. And then they teach you a trade and allow you to enjoy the profits as a person and as a community. And then consider how your self-worth and motivation would grow so that you could extend this family and all its blessings to the next weary traveler. Imagine the tears of joy, the exuberant laughter and levity, and the overwhelming peace that would flood over you.

That's real good news; and it's been the call and work of the church in all times, to work toward new and beautiful expressions of God's kingdom.

Stories like these give us a picture of why we choose to follow Jesus in the ways we do. We get to be artists, free to create new songs of God's kingdom for all to hear, hopefully inspiring other artists to be free to create their own songs of the kingdom.

Act Two

ARCHAEOLOGY, ARTISTRY, AND ARCHITECTURE

The Kingdom Hidden in the City

The kingdom of heaven is like treasure hidden in a field.
When a man found it, he hid it again, and then in his
joy went and sold all he had and bought that field.
MATTHEW 13:44

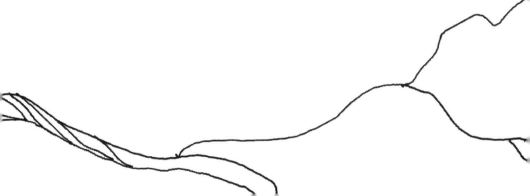

One night in Birmingham, a young family came over to visit us (the McCalls). The adults were all sharing a bottle of Two Buck Chuck from Trader Joe's and reflecting on life, kids, and faith. After some time, the couple asked us if we missed church. Even though I understood the premise of the question, I asked what they meant, and over the next couple of hours, we found ourselves waist-deep into talking about this "other way" of being church. I told them, "Sure, there are things I miss about all sorts of environments I've previously functioned in: my childhood home, my public school, my first year of dating my wife, or my years of being involved in the weekly rhythm of church gatherings. But as I've expanded my paradigm of life, education, love, and community, I've also expanded my view of church. Church is *life* to me now. Church happens in my home, my workplace, and my social spaces; and it includes intentional times, activities, and conversations, as well as spontaneous times, activities, and conversations. Usually it happens in a natural context, where our kids and others in the faith community are with us as we do life and mission together. It's almost like we have too much church sometimes!"

All night long, this couple leaned into the conversation and seemed not only inspired but altogether surprised, as if this was an option they had never considered.

IS THERE SOMETHING MORE?

Think of how many things we just keep doing because we aren't aware of another option. Church as a once-a-week Sunday experience may have prevented millions of people from actually living as Christ-followers.

We know one pastor who, every Monday, prepares and video-records his sermon for the following weekend and then, on Sunday, walks down to participate in a small Anglican community by his house. He told us he hadn't been to his own megachurch services for two years! Another friend gave up his salary, sold his church building, and disbanded his weekend gatherings to facilitate a network of house churches. His lament is that not only is he broke, but also that most of his house church leaders don't actually want to open their homes, and some are now finding other weekend services to attend. Another friend leads a cybercommunity of more than four thousand people, and he's never met any of them personally. He senses good things are happening but admits he has no way of knowing for sure. One friend preaches for eighty widows because they pay him $140,000 a year and he only sees them on Sunday. He golfs for the rest of his time and now has a 6 handicap. One friend who left his church leadership role to become president of a certain denomination shared that all he's done for two years is manage lawsuits and church closures. "I didn't sign up for this," he told us. "Or at least it's not what I thought this job would be."

These anecdotes might seem either like aberrations or like weird and possibly creative options. But regardless of whether you find them inspiring or lamentable, don't miss the glaring commonality. All of these different pictures of church still overwhelmingly orbit around how to teach and gather people.

We're bringing this up not to make fun of those involved or to deconstruct just for the sake of tearing down. We're simply raising this issue to ask whether anyone outside the church cares at all or considers any of our gathered teaching times relevant. And personally, we wonder how many leaders of "once a week" church (in big or microforms), feel exhausted, frustrated, overburdened, and limited.

Most leaders who bring everyone together for a weekly service—regardless of their format—seem to be experiencing burnout. And from the conversations we've had, pastors in the microchurch movements are just as burned out as the megachurch leaders. They still feel that real life is separate from their religious life.

This is why the gospel—the "good news"—must be the ultimate hermeneutic by which we evaluate our critique of church in any form, especially our own. How do we do this? We simply ask ourselves, "Is this good news for me? Am I fulfilled, close to God, about his business, and peaceful in my experience of following Jesus into mission?" Obviously, much of "following him" pulls us into things that don't always feel good or aren't that enjoyable; that's not what we are talking about. We're talking about whether we have the genuine sense that our holistically focused life, bent on leveraging all we are for God, is both personally invigorating and without the angst we might have felt in a more inherited, Sunday-centric mode of church. Another way to judge this is by whether your spouse and children love the way you do life and faith as a family. Trust us; you'll know if it is good news to them!

We don't think there's anything wrong with mega or micro, video or cyber, gathered or scattered, house or weekend church. Each of those experiences is fine for those who want what is being delivered. In other words, if someone leads or partakes in any form of church and genuinely feels it is driving them naturally toward the life and mission of God, then for them, that is good news. But for many, it is not, and other options need to be offered. For us, in the brave city camp, we have come to call teaching and gathering settings "tables," just like every other "table" in the ecosystem. (More on this later.) Teaching and gathering are important concepts and practices, but no more important than any other aspect of life.

What if the options Jesus offers go way beyond teaching and gathering? What if Taylor and Lindsey's meeting with the couple in Birmingham reflects more of an emerging freedom people can discover when church is all of life? And please don't hear what we are not saying. We don't believe *life* is the same as *church*. But we do believe that millions attend church without ever letting it affect much about their lives. The grace of God allows for a more recreational option when following Jesus, but for sure, he doesn't call us to that kind of life. Quoting the Cretan philosopher Epimenides, Paul said "'In him we live and move and have our being'" (Acts 17:28). This seems to suggest that if you find two or three friends and you are following Jesus together, he's with you and can build his church with your rag-tag, sold-out little team. Thus, all of life, if lived in the context of a community of missionaries, is church!

JESUS IN THE WILD

Recently our family (the McCalls) went on a three-week western excursion. We made our way through Kansas and Nebraska, which was about as exciting as watching paint dry. But then we hit Wyoming, and everything changed. It was as if we had been transported to an ancient land, untouched by industry. We marveled at vast open plains, mountain range after mountain range, and lakes that almost looked like paintings in the photographs we took. We saw the Tetons, swam in Jenny Lake, and hiked in Yellowstone and Paradise Valley. It was unforgettable.

None of us had ever been to this part of the country, so when we were planning the trip, and even along the ride, we talked about all the things we wanted to see and experience. And one thing we read about, and heard from friends, is how amazing and terrifying it can be to see a bear in the wild. So, naturally, that went near the top of our list. We had to see a bear.

Now don't get me wrong: The buffalo were amazing. The elk, the moose, all the different wildlife—so cool. But the bear was king. The bear was what we were looking for. Every day, we would hear about a bear sighting that we had just missed. Some hikers saw one five minutes ahead of us on a trail; others saw one on the shore of a mountain lake; and we heard that one even moseyed into a nearby campsite looking for food. But we were always a few steps behind.

Then it happened. On our last night in Yellowstone, we were exhausted and hungry. The sun was going down, and we had been hiking and traveling throughout this massive two-million-acre park for four days. We were driving back to our campground, and I saw someone on the side of the road with a pair of binoculars. Beside him was a little boy, throwing his hands up in the air as if his team had just hit the winning shot. Something told me this wasn't just a buffalo they were watching. I whipped the car into a parking spot and peered out into a huge field called Hayden Valley and, about three hundred yards away, I spied a large figure moving beside a smaller one. The kid shouted out, "It's a grizzly and her cub!" We all jumped out of the vehicle. I can't explain why this thing was so mesmerizing. We just stood there, watching. Before we knew it, more than a hundred people were standing on the edge of the field, watching these bears. Everyone was in awe.

Eventually, we headed back to camp and went to sleep. Ironically, the next morning, as we left Yellowstone to begin our trek home, we saw signs for a bear and wolf exhibit—where we could see the animals up close and risk-free. It cost a pretty penny for all seven of us to go in, but we did.

But the strangest thing happened. Just the day before, a huge crowd of people stood for what seemed like an hour, watching a bear and her cub from two to three football fields away. Now, we were twelve feet from two massive grizzlies, protected by a fence and a moat-like chasm that would've been impossible for them (or us) to cross. I looked at my kids and my wife, and even the ten or so people around me, and no one was really that interested. I mean, it was fun for a minute. It had its impact, of sorts. But shortly after we walked up, all five of my kids wanted to go over to this lame playground a few feet away, and even I was bored. We stayed for a few more minutes, complained about the money we had just dropped for this letdown, and went on our way.

After a few hours of thinking about this whole experience, I realized what had just happened. A little more than twenty years ago, I encountered Jesus "in the wild"—a Jesus that could not be controlled. He wasn't predictable or particularly safe, but I couldn't take my eyes off him. I became completely obsessed with his ways. His glory. His wildness. I had to follow him. And it wasn't even a sacrifice. It didn't even feel like faith. It felt like a secret; as if I'd been let in on something, and I had to tell everyone about it. For the first several years, I was told that the Jesus I encountered could be found in weekly exhibits. And when I would go, I couldn't understand it, because I would see him—or at least a very domesticated, safe, and predictable version of him—and it would leave me somewhat bored. I tried to make the best of it, but if I'm honest, this version of Jesus just wasn't really worth following to me.

The thing about this wild bear, and the thing about this wild Jesus, is they can always be found in their natural habitat. Jesus is out there among the poor and the outcast; he's with the fatherless and the oppressed, and in the kingdom cities that are crafted under his reign. But he can't be boxed, he can't be domesticated, and he can't be predicted. As Mr. Beaver notes of Aslan, the central Jesus-figure in C. S. Lewis's fictional *Chronicles of Narnia* series, "'Course he isn't safe, but he's good."[1]

There will always be those who prefer to approach the bear on their own terms and love the safer, more domesticated, animal. My youngest daughter made it very clear that she preferred the exhibit; the bear in the wild scared her. She didn't know what he would do, and she didn't like the lengths we had to go to to see him. Even though the boxed-in bear didn't keep her attention for very long, she felt better about him. And this is how many people tend to approach Jesus. I don't know if it's fear, the unknown, or if they just never had a genuine wilderness encounter with him. But once you see Jesus in the wild, you know in your heart that this other version of him—the one that you can just come and observe week after week in a manufactured, man-made way—just doesn't cut it.

THE KINGDOM EXPANDING WITHIN US

The kingdom of God seems to be a habitat that Jesus allows to coexist alongside the physical kingdoms of our day. Thus, we can always find evidence of both heavenly and worldly kingdoms. There are "bears" everywhere. The difference is not whether a bear is real or fake but rather whether the bear is in its natural habitat, being what it was designed to be.

In Luke 17:20–21, a Pharisee asks Jesus when the kingdom of God would come, and Jesus replies, "The coming of the kingdom of God is not something that can be observed, nor will people say, 'Here it is,' or 'There it is,' because the kingdom of God is in your midst." Much of this story is about Jesus' return, but there's more to it. *The Passion Translation*, which uses the Aramaic street lingo of the day, phrases Jesus' words this way: "God's kingdom does not come simply by *obeying principles* or waiting for signs. The kingdom is not discovered in one place or another, for God's kingdom realm is already expanding within some of you."

It's interesting that in Matthew 16, Jesus says he will give us the "keys to the kingdom" (v. 19), and in Luke 12 he asks us to "seek the kingdom" (v. 31) and says that the "Father has been pleased to give you the kingdom" (v. 32). But nowhere does he tell us that we will ever be able to point to one specific place and say, "Hey, here it is" because the kingdom is everywhere around us and within us. Even more importantly, we can't find a place where Jesus or the other New Testament writers ever tell us to "build" the kingdom. It's already been built, and all we have to do is look for it, seek it, uncover it, and, like an artist, chip away all that's *not it* to reveal it.

This is a critical understanding because, in modern-day ministry, we love to tell people where the kingdom can be found. "Come to our 10 a.m. service or our Thursday night small group, and you'll experience God," we might say. And the people come and even pay their tithe. Yet when they get back in the minivan, the kids and the adults often agree it wasn't what they were looking for.

The most important thing to focus on is that the kingdom is not something we *make* or *build* or *produce*. The kingdom is just there, all the time; and it does produce things, but what the kingdom produces must fit in the habitat for which it was designed, or it won't have its intended result. Even more, if we think kingdom growth shows up as a single thing in a moment, we'll miss the joy of the kingdom along the way. And the craziest thought is that the kingdom only expands as it expands within us. Let that settle in.

It's not that we *build* the kingdom, but that the kingdom *is being built* through the work God is doing in us, both in holiness but also in the ideas we come up with and the obedience we exhibit as we put our hand to the plow. So, since God is at work in us, we do "works" that are of his kingdom, but the works themselves are not the kingdom. The coffee shops and restaurants, the justice efforts, the house churches, and the parties are not the kingdom, but the kingdom reveals itself in us and these environments. The ways of the kingdom inhabit and have an influence *upon* and *in* all these things, but never make the mistake of thinking we make the kingdom happen. It might seem like splitting hairs, but if you've been involved in any of these environments or activities, you know the kingdom isn't always obvious, and we can quickly lose our way and put emphasis only on things we see. However, the kingdom is at work, regardless of its visible reality to us.

As Matthew 13 showed us, the kingdom is the treasure in the field. The treasure has always been there, waiting to be uncovered. But we must sell everything we own to "find" it. When Michelangelo was asked about his sculptures, he said, "Every block of stone has a statue inside it, and it is the task of the sculptor to discover it."[2] Imagine the time, patience, and obsession it must have taken for him to finally see the treasure in the stone, not to mention the work required to uncover it. We are the sculptors, the artists, the city builders, chipping away at the very heart of the world's empire, in essence following all the lessons Jesus taught. And in that chipping away, we find the treasure, uncover it, and then share the good news with others that the kingdom is here, and they're welcomed into it.

We'll talk more about metrics later, but here is where we need to have a serious discussion about doing away with the commonly accepted metrics of "success" or "best practices" or "growth" as indicators of kingdom fruit. Instead of counting anything, we suggest you help people set their antennae for God's activity and to simply rejoice when they detect it. Remember our discussion of "moments, not formulas" in act one? It's those moments that become indicators in this regard. For example:

- At a nice dinner with friends around some great food and drink with some perfect light jazz playing. When everyone is relaxed and tangibly enjoying each other's friendship, deep, thoughtful, and even challenging questions are posed, and struggles are shared and encouraged.
- At a point of suffering, when the community rallies and cares for one another just like you read about in the book of Acts and you think, "Wow their story is our story."
- While working on a common project to start a business or "thing," and you're not quite sure how it will end up or even if it will do any good, and none of your donors or investors seem to get the nebulous vision, but for some reason, you just feel led to try it. It works, and what you imagined gets fulfilled and people are blessed.

These are signs that the kingdom is not only around you but is also expanding within you. Still, the metrics are more like breadcrumbs. You just follow them. When you can learn to enjoy the mystery and embrace the journey, that's when the fun starts.

Two things to remember: First, whatever God leads you to do must be organic, healthy, and grown in the way God designed things to grow. And second, whatever he leads you to architect must be in the wild and not become domesticated and safe.

ARCHEOLOGY, ARTISTRY, AND ARCHITECTURE

When we think of church as all of life in a particular city, we often get asked if there are specific things we should focus on or do. We can't tell you exactly what those things are, but the answer is a rousing yes! Just as in life, you focus on and prioritize some activities over others, so intentionality is a must if we are to be about our Father's business. But remember, we don't build the kingdom. The kingdom is already there. And we don't build the church. That's God's job. What we do is uncover the kingdom that is already there, hidden in the city, to create new songs and new works that reveal God's heart.

Not only have we not been called to build the kingdom on earth, but we also actually messed it up. We didn't tend it well. And like an old, abandoned property, the vines, dirt, and debris have overgrown and covered up the kingdom in our cities. The vines include the dominant power structures of religion, empire, and the human condition of sin that seeks to choke out the kingdom of God. When we come in with our conquering mindset and just start constructing things, we build on a faulty foundation, like a contractor who covers up mold with new drywall. We must first sniff around and get a sense of the story and the people God has used in ways we can't understand, long before we got there. More times than not, it's their prayers that drew us there. We need to think about being archaeologists, artists, and architects. It's important to think in new terms like this because if we don't, we often take a posture that is too aggressive and miss key nuances that are critical.

First, think *archaeology*. We must shed this conquering spirit and instead come in as simple searchers and scientists of the kingdom, ready to experiment and innovate as we uncover the beauty that's been hidden. Often, that beauty can be found among the poor—those who've been forgotten by all but Jesus. They are often seen as problems to fix, but in reality, God uses them to fix us, teaching us things such as community, interdependency, and generosity. As we uncover the kingdom in our city, we uncover God's true heart. Although we firmly believe that God leans toward the poor and hurting, we also believe he is just as passionate about beautiful community spaces to eat, drink, party, or engage in quiet intercessory prayer.

Next, think *artistry*. As God's heart expands in us, new priorities grow in our hearts, and we respond by creating things we think will help and heal. Because the kingdom is not built on strategy or modern-day growth metrics, we must look for something less measurable, more mystical, yet still tangible. As the artists, we create and innovate. In college, I (Taylor) took several songwriting courses as a part of my degree. The songs that have stuck with me to this day are the ones that had little to nothing to do with the prescriptive elements of a "sellable" song. The chord structures and lyrical simplicity found within a typical three-minute and fifteen-second radio song, although fun to sing along to in the car, never inspired me or captured my interest. But when the true artists would talk about elements and nuances such as passion, authenticity, real-life experience, and grit, I felt motivated. Similarly, the plug-and-play method of modern-day church planting reminds me of the people who just want radio airtime: "Give me the song I need to sing to be successful." Church-planting conferences today seem more like karaoke shows than writers' rounds. Where's the artistry, the listening, the waiting? Where's the desperation for the song that is truly inspired by something outside of you? This takes time, experience, and, unfortunately, pain. It takes patience and longing. In these quiet and sometimes lonely places we really begin to hear from God, and we can't help but begin to sing the song he's giving us.

And, think *architecture*. From the listening and longing, actual *structures* emerge—including innovative spaces, new experiences, and well-crafted tables for your city. God might spark thoughts of places where others can come to find a nice drink, an after-school refuge, or a family to eat with. Places where seekers feel hope again. Restaurants, gyms, pubs, homes, or barber shops. There's no strict framework to determine which structures to build; it's just a matter of acting with honesty and authenticity in the pursuit and with anticipation of some level of "fruitfulness." Kingdom architecture often looks like actual architecture, because physical things can be used to reveal the supernatural beauty of the kingdom; but the architecture of the things built or renovated should connect into the story of your context and relate to the longings of the people in your city. This can (and probably should) take years. And despite what a church-planting coach might say, these are things only your Father can teach you.

The goal is to process what church, as all of life, might feel like, instead of building teaching centers, programs, or worship gatherings. None of those are bad, but when we see ourselves as dispensers of religious goods and services, we almost always head toward the same thing we've been doing for the last 1,700 years. But if we think of ourselves as archaeologists, artists, and architects, it tends to activate our curiosity, passion, and creativity. And it begs us to ask the questions and find the solutions that our lost world is trying to get answers to and get help with. We may not always succeed, but we will wake up in the morning with a quest and a work ethic that might be a game-changer.

"GOOD BUT NOT SAFE"

Earlier in this act we noted, as C. S. Lewis penned it, that Jesus isn't safe, but he is good. As the kingdom is uncovered, God's heart is revealed, tables of belonging are built, and the towns and cities you live in will be changed—not from a political position of power but as an alternative city and kingdom ecosystem to which people slowly transfer their allegiance because of what they see happening on the streets. This is the good work of God revealing and growing his kingdom within a city. But this is not "safe" work. This work takes bravery.

When Jesus taught us to turn the other cheek (Matthew 5:39), he wasn't advocating for a cowardly response to big Roman thugs (his listeners' enemies) randomly trying to humiliate you with an unwarranted backhand across the face. Of course, you could fight back—but you would swiftly die. Jesus didn't tell us to run away either, as if you only had a fight-or-flight option. To turn the other cheek was a third option: a non-violent, subversive form of resistance that actually looks like bravery.

Imagine, you're walking down the street with your family and some other families you know. Some Roman military guy arrogantly strolls up to you, hassles you verbally, and then, without warning, slaps you—just because he can. In front of your children and other shocked onlookers, you square back up, look the abuser in the face, and then wink and subtly turn your face slightly to the left while never breaking eye contact as if to say, "You forgot this side of my face." That's what Jesus was asking his students to do: not cower, not kowtow, not attack, but simply to straighten up and stand firm against the dominant system while people watch. It isn't just non-violence but stern resolve and confidence that even if someone takes your life, you'll still be the winner.

Now imagine hundreds and thousands taking on this approach in front of thousands of onlookers and then hearing that these same Jesus-people sell their possessions, care for anyone in need, constantly show hospitality to strangers and foreigners, and seem to approach any form of death with a wink and a smile. What you have is the makings of a form of resistance that can wipe out the Romans—or any power, for that matter.

You want to make us walk a mile with you? Well, when you get tired, we'll offer to go another mile. If you want us to give you a coat, we'll throw in our shirts too. For years, this has been misunderstood as humble kindness, but we like to call it "subtle subversion."

In teaching this kind of response, Jesus was revealing another city, with new laws, new ethics, and new private and public goals. The overarching objective was to subvert and dominate evil.

So it can be in our day. Kingdom-oriented cities are the most holistic form of resistance; a subtle subversion of the worldly powers dominating the cities of Portland, Pittsburgh, or New Orleans. We don't shrink back, and we don't strike out. We simply stand firm and offer an alternative framework within which to live. And maybe we do even more.

In a fascinating video teaching, American theologian Dr. Michael Heiser teaches on an often-mistranslated passage in

Matthew 16.[3] Jesus is with his disciples in Caesarea Philippi at the foot of Mount Hermon. In Old Testament times, this location featured a massive rock face, well-known for its geological significance. But Mount Hermon was more prominently recognized as the epicenter of pagan worship. It was the location of the Temple of Zeus as well as substantial shrines dedicated to Baal. Because of the false worship and pagan rituals that took place in this location, it became known as "The Gates of Hell."

In this classic interplay between Jesus and Peter, Jesus tells Peter, "On this rock I will build my church, and the gates of hell shall not prevail against it" (Matthew 16:18 ESV). We often interpret this as Jesus giving a general word of encouragement that Satan and his workers will never prevail against his church. And many think that he is telling Peter that he is the actual rock upon which the entire church will be built (the classic teaching of Catholicism). But it's far more compelling than that. Jesus is saying, "Friends, we're standing on the center of idol worship and false gods. So right here, on this very rock of idol worship, these gates of hell, we will now reestablish and restore the kingdom of God. We are occupying their space. We are taking over where they have so freely lied and deceived people for centuries."

Friends, this is huge for us to understand, especially when we establish new works of the kingdom. Much of our present-day church planting has been more like franchising Chick-fil-A into the nicer suburbs, where we are sure we'll always have a long line waiting for our consumer goods. Jesus is turning that on its head. He's saying that if we establish anything, it should be a direct assault upon any and all spirits of the day that deceive people into believing in false hopes and false gods. We are not a defensive church. We are always on the offensive, just more subtly and wisely. We are definitely not afraid or circling the wagons trying to stay alive.

Practically this means that when we, "the church," innovate new works, they should be entities that stand in the pathway of evil. If we renovate old buildings that have been boarded up for years and create places of community, laughter, joy, camaraderie, and commerce, we are challenging the spirit of loss, depression, recession, and loneliness. When we initiate youth sports teams or leagues, we are coming against family curses of fatherlessness. When we help others start new businesses, we are coming against poverty and all the ills that come from a lack of basic needs and dignity. When we renovate our backyards so that the entire neighborhood has a place to connect, we are literally forging and forming an outpost of kingdom love and connection. When we buy an old dive bar and keep it that way, but staff it and fill it with new patrons who are there intentionally to love on the locals, we are poking Satan in the eye. We're standing on his rock and tearing down his places of false worship.

Here's the truth: Not everything we do will work, or at least work in the way we think it should. Sometimes our businesses will fail. Sometimes we won't be able to get the funding to support the youth sports team. Sometimes a leader will get sick or die, and their kingdom work will stop. In these times, remember the main reason we dive deep into these issues and endeavors isn't because they always work. We do it because our lives are to be a precursor of things to come. Brave cities reflect and model the great eschatological reality that someday the tables will be filled, and everyone will have a home.

Theologian Walter Wink taught about this "third way," and about how the traditional approach to opposing evil was inadequate.[4] He points to the brilliant subversion that happens through God's people as they silently, humbly live the kingdom in community, like the subterranean churches during the Dark Ages, or the American Black church that slowly, carefully crafted a society within the society of slavery in which they were subjected. They came up with their own music—both celebration and dirges—with unique cadences that would lift their souls amidst the weight of tyranny and oppression. When Black churches finally emerged after the American Civil War, they established their own way of linking commerce, community, liturgy, cuisine, and arts, all through the church.

For example, the often-overlooked story of the Greenwood

District (also known as "Black Wall Street") at the heart of the tragic Tulsa race massacre from May 31–June 1, 1921, illustrates the power of a church integrated in all facets of life. The Greenwood District represented the most comprehensive city-building project our country has seen, and the church was at its center. Although it was deliberately burned to the ground, the spirit of the church continued to roll on until the civil rights movement of the '60s.

Is racism dead? Of course not, but did the church in Tulsa subvert the system of slavery? Of course, it did. Did the small band of Christians occupied by Rome eventually subvert Rome? Yes, they did. Could brave cities, over time, subvert the worldly systems plaguing our society today by slowly revealing the kingdom of God that has been hidden? Of course. Will we all see the results of our work? Of course not, but we think the repeated story of the church as a brave city throughout history gives us the best way to live and find the purpose we are all seeking.

These and many more stories give us tangible examples to shoot for, pray for, and work for. The goal of all of it, yes, is to glorify God and make him known, but even more practically, it is to subvert the present powers and principalities, the systemic systems and spiritual strongholds that hold cities down. Now imagine every city having a few brave cities in them. Not only would these be amazing ecosystems within which to grow our own families, but they might even, like the early church, turn entire regions on their heads (Acts 17:6). How did that happen? Jesus' followers believed that when, in Matthew 16, he gave them the keys to the kingdom and the ability to bind and loose, it would happen! It did happen in Rome. It's happened throughout history. It is not a pipe dream!

SO, IS THIS CHURCH?

Those of us who have gotten used to the safe, domesticated, predictable, easily identifiable expressions of the church are going to have a harder time accepting the wilder, less predictable, more hidden expressions of the church. On a coaching call with another kingdom ecosystem leader from Dublin, Ireland, we were asked how we in Alton handle the questions of whether or not we are really church. That leader said a person asked him, "How are you even legit?"

In every kingdom ecosystem we've studied or coached, we've found that the leaders of those movements always talk about the judgment they receive from other church leaders about the validity of their movement as a "church." Can you really call this a church if you don't have consistent weekend services? Can it really be a church if people in the movement don't agree on every doctrinal position? Can it really be a church if, if, if?

Coupled with the judgment is an appreciation for what these movements do. Because these kingdom ecosystems often center around the margins and the marginalized, they are often viewed like the Salvation Army or other "doing-good" groups and are thus considered an asset to the cities they serve. They tend to be deeply respected as creative missionary expressions—but not as "churches."

As we've implied before, we don't believe (as some do) that church is just hanging out on a lake with your dog and a few friends. We see the totality of Jesus, Paul, Peter, John, and other New Testament writers filling in a much fuller picture of a community on mission, held together by their common love of Jesus. So please don't think we are minimizing the beauty and fullness of the church. But we'd like to give you a permission slip so that you can move forward with some blessing as you push away from the centrist ideals of what church is.

Interestingly, Jesus only mentioned the word "church" twice (Matthew 16:18; Matthew 18:15,17), so that alone shows he's not interested in providing a textbook on the subject. Besides these two passages that use the word "church," the other more accurate and prophetic description Jesus used for his community was a "city on a hill" (Matthew 5:14–16). God's people become something that is visible, shining in the darkness, accessible to those looking for it. It doesn't, however, support the notion that the church is some political juggernaut that stands above the peasant class, keeping watch as the moral majority or sin police. It literally meant a light amid the darkness, like a lighthouse guiding wandering ships into a safe harbor.

Jesus gave very little instruction on how we should organize, what traditions we should make or uphold, what doctrines we should create, what worship style or frequency we should adopt, or, quite frankly, how to achieve any of the modern-day metrics we accept as normative for being a church. Instead, Jesus gave us the foundational gospel concept of freedom and lordship for life in the kingdom of God. The truth of Christ's resurrection and the promise of the Holy Spirit is our ultimate joy and strength, helping us to keep going, as we know we have the final victory. Our primary activity or work is uncovering, architecting, and artistically crafting tables of God's presence as we invite others into this kingdom life. The primary medium for all this goodness to be accomplished and enjoyed is his community, his church. So the church has a central gospel and purpose, but everything else related to how the church operates can be interpreted and practiced in various ways.

Yes, we agree it might have been easier if Jesus had been more prescriptive about the church he said he came to die for. Why didn't he just tell us what to do, how to do it, and how to grow it? Just like my (Taylor) songwriting mentors, Jesus wanted us free to go and create, to relax on the things that don't matter much, and to work hard on the things that mean everything. Remember, when Jesus dropped the seven woes in Matthew 23:13–32, he acknowledged that the Pharisees and teachers of the law were focused on silly stuff while neglecting the game-changers of justice and mercy. He knew his community—his big "C" church—needed all the little communities to look different in order to catch the unique nuances each context requires. He wanted his church to be free and freely given to the world.

We must remember that God has only one church. In any city, there are different expressions related to location, size, and style that reflect unique thumbprints of diversity. But in Alton, there is only one church. In America, there is only one church. Worldwide, there is only one church. So asking if our strange, experimental expressions are legitimate forms of church is to ask the wrong question. In our expression in Alton, we focus on deep life-discipleship so we can develop sold-out missionaries who live a rhythm of life together where they share all things, build kingdom tables together, and gather more than weekly to talk about Scripture, the kingdom, and how to make their lives more like Jesus. We do this mission in plain view of our children, often share the story of Jesus and the kingdom with many people who ask, and collectively build a story that causes both believers and unbelievers to respect and appreciate our presence in the city. I would think most would agree that that's a "pretty dang good church." But, because we don't have a public church name or a consistent weekly "all together" gathering, people struggle to give us "church" status. When people have been brought up to see church as a place you go or a brand you try to proliferate, non-institutional forms just look weird. But we are not only an expression of church; we are also a part of the larger global church. It's just that we have a more intentional rhythm and focus on bettering our city and helping people to dig and find the kingdom through justice works, enterprise, and homes of intention.

WHAT *DO* WE CALL THIS?

Since the beginning, disciples of Jesus identified themselves as a family together in local communities. Initially, it appears that they struggled to put a name to their localized expressions and even the larger movement, because they were often in stealth or undercover mode. We should not let this go unnoticed or fail to learn from it.

As we think about identifying the ministries we are dreaming about, the language we use is important. When "churches" were mentioned in the New Testament, it was almost always as a unique community inside an actual city. Paul, addressing the church in Rome, said, "To all in Rome who are loved by God and called to be his holy people" (Romans 1:7). To the church in Corinth, he said, "To the church of God in Corinth" (1 Corinthians 1:2). Other letters say, "To God's holy people in Ephesus" (Ephesians 1:1), "To God's holy people in Christ Jesus in Philippi" (Philippians 1:1), and, "To God's elect, exiles scattered throughout the province of Pontus, Galatia, Cappadocia, Asia and Bithynia" (1 Peter 1:1). Clearly, in those days, people didn't identify themselves by their brand of the Christian sect. Instead, they identified themselves by the cities they lived in—or maybe more specifically, the houses inside the cities, like Phoebe's home. For the first three hundred years, they didn't have buildings that carried their brand name. They either referenced the home or city as their identifier.

Thus, it seems intuitive that the ecosystems we reference are creating names for their movements that reflect their common mission or relational network inside their city. They almost invariably see themselves as part of the church in their city, but their unique thumbprint represents a distinct posture or presence there. Thus, they can build together alongside those they partner with.

Lantern Network, Common Thread, Well Built City, Love City, BlueHouse, Good Hood, just to name a few, all picked names that allow for all sorts of works, activities, and church expressions. But whereas many churches pick names to attract anyone and everyone, kingdom ecosystem names often create a filter so that church shoppers, passive attendees, and consumers of religious goods and services won't find them. We don't mean you shouldn't dream or hope for thousands to be a part of your ecosystem, but we think you'll be healthier, and your city will be more effectively changed, if you shoot for somewhere between twenty to a hundred missionaries in your movement. Of course, many more, and many thousands, may be touched by the works of the smaller number, but we think it's best to focus on the missionaries and their development. And truthfully, as more come, more will naturally be sent out to other places. Then those missionaries can focus on the work of revealing the kingdom to *their* cities.

We should probably state right here that we do have hopes, dreams, and clear aspirations for areas of growth and movement. But our "metrics," if you will, are simple because we think the kingdom works best when taking small, reproducible, and faithful steps. (God always seemed to winnow down the army he needed for his fight.) We are bringing this up not to be avant-garde or counter-cultural, but instead as a reminder not to be weighed down or to create standards that can't be lived up to. That's not edgy; it's just ancient.

God's people of today and tomorrow will identify themselves in strange and simple ways, but their identity must not be the name of a building where they attend a weekend church service.

NEVER STOP SEARCHING FOR TREASURE

Hopefully, this gives you just enough foundation to feel your way through the rest of this book. Try not to figure out too much ahead of time. For most ecosystems, it's like finding bread on the trail as you wander in the wilderness of a mission. But as you slowly uncover the kingdom, people will slowly build things that matter, and tables will be added where people will find new life in the kingdom.

We've focused several times in this act on Matthew 13 where Jesus says the kingdom is like a treasure. Treasure is what men and women search for. If you've ever seen the Taylor Sheridan masterpiece *1883*, you'll remember it as the story of an immigrant community trying to reach the Pacific Coast.[5] Most of the episodes expose the incredible ordeal of heading west, where everything was unknown and dangerous. In each installment, you'd justifiably wonder why they kept pushing ahead instead of just hunkering down and settling—as "settlers" do. But the inspiration was in their pioneering and courageous hope of finding something like a treasure. Yes, many died, but some made it, the West was born, and future generations got to enjoy the fruit of their efforts. So, if you've tried and gotten struck by some arrows, faced some adversity, and even lost some people along the way, we hope our stories will reignite the pioneer-builder spirit in you and that you'll keep searching for the kingdom treasure buried in your city.

Act Three

KINGDOM ECOSYSTEMS

There's Something in the Dirt

Unless a kernel of wheat falls to the ground and dies,
it remains only a single seed.
JOHN 12:24

As [the farmer] was scattering the seed … some fell on rocky places.
MATTHEW 13:4–5

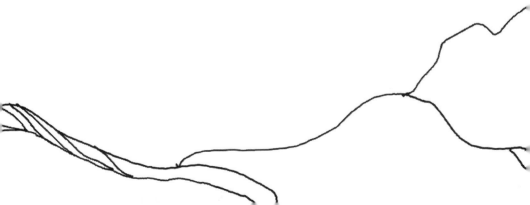

A little-known fact about me (Hugh) is that I love cooking. Even more, I love grocery shopping. I know most people can't stand it, but I love hunting for unique ingredients to make fantastic food for the tribe. But when our oldest daughter, Alli, was in late high school and college, we went through a five-year dark spell that turned my love of cooking into despair. Everything seemed to make her sick, nauseous, and "loose in the caboose," as they say. Besides the pain of watching her in constant agony, our family had to all but stop going out to eat, and then my love of grocery shopping was killed by her sending me to the store with lists like, "Probiotic oat milk, spirulina, wheatgrass, orchid fungi, gravel root, and pine bark extract."

I hated trying to find these ingredients, and I didn't think they were fit for consumption. Alli couldn't eat gluten, which was a problem because gluten is a major ingredient in some of my favorite foods, like bread and pasta. Alli wouldn't touch meat and would get really upset with me when we'd be driving by a pasture full of cows, and I'd say, "Those cows look delicious." At first, I thought the sickness was mostly in her head. But as I started to learn more about organics and saw the statistics on how many people now suffer from chronic dietary health issues, I couldn't avoid the reality that something is wrong with our food, and it is adversely impacting our health.

The study of organics is based on soil, which is the most complex ecosystem in the world—far more complex than even our oceans. Healthy soil is filled with thousands of microorganisms. You can actually smell good soil and feel the warmth it emits as all these beautifully complex organisms interact. Remember back in the day when you didn't worry if your kids ingested some dirt? Yep, it was okay because it used to be safe. I've even read studies on trauma and depression therapy that involve people standing barefoot in healthy soil because the microorganisms in our bodies respond immediately to all that health and goodness.

But all over the world, our soils are turning into lifeless dirt. Over the past 150 years, we have depleted more than half of the world's agricultural topsoil using farming practices based on high yields or getting produce grown as fast as possible.[1] If nothing changes, we will have no growing soil in the future.

Interestingly, you can still grow stuff in this lifeless dirt. But to do it, you must genetically modify the seeds so that when you've loaded up the dead soil with pesticides, growth hormones, and other chemicals, the seeds can still grow, even if everything else around the seed dies. This is one of the reasons so many people today get sick from the foods they eat. This preventable global issue is literally a matter of the ecosystem dying beneath our feet.

Jesus understood the importance of soil, which is why he often spoke about dirt, soil, and fruit, warning that bad soil produces bad crops, bad crops do not produce good fruit, and things that do not bear good fruit will wither away and be thrown into the fire. The prophets Daniel and Ezekiel both used trees as a metaphor to describe the difference between those who bear lasting fruit and those who bear fruit quickly but are easily uprooted. In Daniel chapter 4, Nebuchadnezzar is shown his kingdom ecosystem in a dream as a very large tree benefitting everyone. But God takes note of his self-serving actions and his insatiable empire-building and responds by tearing down the tree (providing a cautionary tale about reckless growth). In Ezekiel chapter 17, we see a vision of God taking a branch of that same tree and replanting it, but this time it is built by the Lord and thus it doesn't get torn down. Unlike the counterfeit ecosystem of Nebuchadnezzar, what God grows always bears fruit and brings benefit to everyone around.

Jesus often used agricultural metaphors because the world at that time understood the direct connection between farming and food. There were no grocery stores or DoorDash delivery services or shortcuts of any kind. People had to align their actions with the reality that poor practices meant poor results; and honest, natural practices produced good fruit. And so, in this act, while we need to talk about what kingdom cities are and how to build them, we first need to talk about the kingdom and how careful we must be about *how* we build and grow, not just *what* we build and grow. We also must settle some issues of what is natural and what is unnatural. Even more importantly, we have to nail down what is the kingdom, what is a mirage, and what is real.

As we said in the last act, we can't tell you exactly how to build your ecosystem. We won't tell you the key to everything is a coffee shop or a business or even justice works. We will just remind you that whatever God leads you to do must be organic, healthy, and grown in the way God designed things to grow. Over the next few pages, we will share some key architectural elements and critical nuances that are essential in forging healthy kingdom ecosystems.

ELEMENTS OF KINGDOM ARCHITECTURE

Just for fun, we thought we'd try to draw a picture of our ecosystem in Alton (see the image on the opposite page).

We find that as we travel to see other ecosystems, there are a lot of similarities and that in almost every context there are benevolent businesses, justice works, and intentional homes in strategic neighborhoods. The picture doesn't show every home, as many are just homes. But as unique families position and leverage their space for the community, these homes become very strategic. When folks ask the most fundamental question of what to start planting, we almost always say it will be a business that the town needs and wants, justice works that specifically target deep areas of brokenness, and strategically incarnational homes. If you at least start there, you're probably going to be planting things that align with Jesus' heart.

Beyond these, below are some of the architectural elements that Jesus builds upon.

LANTERN NETWORK

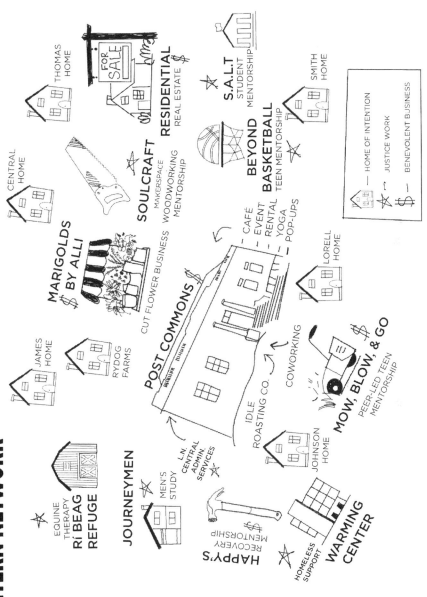

THOMAS HOME

FOR SALE

RESIDENTIAL
REAL ESTATE

S.A.L.T
STUDENT MENTORSHIP

SMITH HOME

CENTRAL HOME

SOULCRAFT
MAKERSPACE
WOODWORKING
MENTORSHIP

BEYOND BASKETBALL
TEEN MENTORSHIP

MARIGOLDS BY ALLI
CUT FLOWER BUSINESS

— CAFÉ
— EVENT
— RENTAL
— YOGA
— POP-UPS

LORELL HOME

JAMES HOME

RYDOG FARMS

POST COMMONS

COWORKING

MOW, BLOW, & GO
PEER-LED TEEN MENTORSHIP

IDLE ROASTING CO.

EQUINE THERAPY
Rí BEAG REFUGE

JOURNEYMEN
MEN'S STUDY

L.N. CENTRAL ADMIN. SERVICES

JOHNSON HOME

HAPPY'S
RECOVERY MENTORSHIP

HOMELESS SUPPORT

WARMING CENTER

— HOME OF INTENTION

— JUSTICE WORK

— BENEVOLENT BUSINESS

Disciples

In the organics movement, the way to restore lifeless dirt back into soil alive with microbes is by planting a "cover crop." A cover crop is exactly what it sounds like—a crop that grows on the surface and improves soil health by preventing erosion, increasing organic matter, promoting microbe activity, controlling weeds, and enhancing pest control.

Think of disciples as the cover crop of the kingdom.

Jesus only had roughly three years to frame his kingdom ecosystem. He came into the lifeless dirt pile of Jewish religion, the Roman empire, and brutal social structures. People were sick of segregation, poverty, war, corruption, legalism, fear, hypocrisy, and hopelessness. He had a lot of work to do in a relatively short amount of time.

The strategy of our day would most likely be to gather as many followers as possible, as quickly as possible, to achieve the biggest impact. But Jesus didn't do that. He invested his time in a select few people, relying on the potential for long-term, exponential growth if their lives could replicate his own. His strategy was to develop the character of a few disciples to eventually reach the whole world. He invested in a cover crop to bring the dead dirt back to life—and it worked.

In other words, Jesus didn't start by planting churches; he planted people. He called them disciples. In Matthew 5, Jesus begins his internship not by teaching his followers how to do or be the church, or how to gain military power, or how to do anything strategic. Instead, he taught them (paraphrasing), "If you are salt and light, everywhere I plant you will become a better place. You'll have better conversations, better families, better neighborhoods, better businesses, better Facebook conversations, better jokes, better community, better food, and yes ... better wine." He focused on embedding discipleship into the dead dirt to create healthy soil again.

Jesus was not just God incarnate; he was the smartest and most strategic person the world has ever seen, and he knew he had to guard against potential kingdom movement killers. Just a note on the word "movement" here. Churches, as far as a localized brand or identity, can cease to exist—whether after a one-hundred-year run or in a sudden implosion after a pastor has a moral failure. When its identity is based on its name or brand, which centers around a Sunday gathering, the church will most likely not be "movemental." Jesus' plan was for everything to be a movement—advancing, going forward, never stalling or shrinking back. (Even losses and deaths usually give movements a spark.) Thus, Jesus' most strategic move was to place this potential in the smallest, most reproducible element of his plan: the disciple. But he wasn't after numbers. He was focused on the individual and collective quality of his followers— the small bands of disciples who would be the actual witnesses to the world of this new kingdom.

Why was this strategic? Because the movement could be killed if the people were advertising, Facebooking, or tweeting their big intentions without a strong grounding in him. The movement could also die a fast death if it was jockeying for political control or leading from a dominant position. All it would take to stop the movement would be the loss of a key leader, a great economic depression, a worldwide pandemic, or a sexual abuse allegation. Anything could take a church down, just like today.

Jesus warned against public religion (Matthew 6:5). He taught his disciples to infiltrate quietly, and to live significant, holy, and loving lives; and in everything, to be so countercultural that people couldn't help but ask for the reason for their hope (Matthew 5). The disciples were everything to Jesus. They were not just numbers in a competition to make more disciples than the next rabbi. Instead, it was all about the quality of one, and then two, and then three disciples who lived on the fringes but changed society at the center ... eventually.

Proverbs 11:10, which is really the foundational text for this

entire book, says, "When the righteous prosper, the city rejoices."
These types of disciples, these "righteous ones," produce so much
good that not only is everyone desperate for their presence but they
also would lament if they ever left town. Could we say the same
for the "church" in its present form? Probably not, but this is why
Jesus doesn't start by calling us to plant churches; instead, he tells
us to plant disciples upon whom he can build his church (Matthew
28:19–20).

Just before our family moved to Alton, I (Taylor) had an
encouraging conversation with the mayor of Birmingham at
a local car wash. I mentioned we would be moving, and the
mayor asked with a concerned voice, "So is the entire network
leaving?" I quickly replied, "No, not at all. They are all still here
and will continue their work. It's just our family moving for a
while." Relieved, the mayor said, "Well, that's good, because
if all your community were to leave, we'd have to raise taxes
to cover all the good you guys are doing in our city." At the
time, the community in Birmingham was less than one hundred
missionaries.

Similarly, just three years into our time in Alton, many locals
and city leaders privately told us how much encouragement and
positive change had happened in our business district because
of what our ecosystem was doing. At the time, we were less than
twenty missionaries.

Maybe now you're getting the picture of why Jesus makes such a
big deal about the single disciple and why he wanted us to focus on
quality and not quantity. He understood that disciples are constantly
being made, so it's not a matter of *whether* we make disciples but
rather of the *quality* of our disciple-making.

This is why Jesus wasn't impressed with the evangelism of his
day. Yes, you read that right. In Matthew 23:15, he told the most
biblically literate, devout, prayerfully committed, highly evangelistic religious leaders that they would travel land and sea to make
even one convert, but then turn them into twice as much a child of

hell as they were. Jesus had no interest in growing a movement if the movement was full of Pharisees.

In Matthew 16:6, he even warned his disciples to watch out for the leaven of the Pharisees. Wow! Don't just watch out for the pharisaical people but also be on your guard for even the slightest pharisaical molecule that can get inside God's kingdom and screw up the whole loaf.

This should stand as a stark warning to anyone wanting to start even the smallest kingdom ecosystem. This is why in Matthew 5, Jesus describes how those who follow him should live and act—and how different it was from the dominant religion, dominant country, or dominant political agenda. He warned that, if we don't live in radically different ways, eventually the cover crop will not be able to bring any nutrients to the table, and the salt (v. 13) will lose its ability to preserve.

Friends, we are there now! There's no debating that pop Christian culture has lost its sway, its market share, and its allure. Over, finished, el done-o! The salt is gone! What's left, in Jesus' words, is for it to be trampled into the hard soil beneath our feet. And the soil is indeed hard as a rock—so hard that seeds won't grow and are easily plucked by the birds (Matthew 13). If the city is to be built, we need soft, rich, amended soil, salted with real disciples.

Convergent Spaces

So, we start with the cover crop, the disciple. Then we consider the need for a central connection or convergent space from which to operate apostolically. These spaces (often reclaimed buildings) prophetically speak of renewal and redemption and are places where people connect, dream, work, partner, share, and live in solidarity with the community. This can be a home, or a set of homes close together, a business or commercial space, or any combination of those. We think that the *person* of peace in Luke 10 can also be a *spirit* of peace that comes over a home, neighborhood, community, or city—and often this spirit of peace is manifested in *spaces* of peace.

Throughout history, there have been places where people of the Jesus movement gathered. These places can be "underground" or above ground. Examples include the first-century home of Priscilla and Aquilla (1 Corinthians 16:19); the monastic community in Glendalough, Ireland; and the ex-slave settlement in Ontario, Canada, where people gathered, connected, and modeled a way of life that grew a kingdom ecosystem. In Alton, our flagship convergent space is known as Post Commons, a renovated 1909 federal post office that now serves as the "living room for Alton." As I (Hugh) write this from Post Commons, it's Saturday morning, and I'm looking at about sixty people having breakfast. Some of our community leaders (missionaries) are walking around talking with folks, others in our team are working in the kitchen or at the barista bar, and many friends who are not yet following Jesus are connecting and enjoying our space.

Regardless of what the space is, there seems to be a great benefit in having a place where people live, work, eat, exercise, build a business, or just share a coffee. The identity is not as a church, but there is a tangible presence of our common work in an area of a city from which God builds out everything. Consider these convergent spaces like a feed store for all the farmers who are tending to soil, or the hardware store for all those contractors or woodworkers building tables, or an airport serving folks as they pass through. Any metaphor works, as long as the space, the work in the space, and the contributors in the space are working for God's good in their town.

Kingdom Economy

What you also find in a kingdom ecosystem is an economy. We're going to spend the entire next act talking about money and mission, but for now, remember that we are creating a kingdom city within a city. Your city, the businesses, governments, and most churches operate in a transactional economy. People pay based on what they think they are getting. It's called the consumer system, and it's not necessarily bad, but it's designed to keep consumers consuming.

In a kingdom ecosystem, money is leveraged in a way that challenges consumerism and grows a sacrificial shared economy so that people get real help. This economy, focused on people, isn't about handouts or putting Band-Aids on issues that will come back next month. A kingdom economy is about sustainability and building businesses that will keep bearing fruit and reinvestment opportunities. So, the business economies in a kingdom ecosystem are not to prop up programs, pay religious salaries, or keep the lights on in buildings that function primarily as worship centers. In a kingdom economy, the "worshiping" community commits and leverages their work, energy, assets, homes, tools, gifts, cash, and creativity to create the quadruple win of helping people, keeping missionaries funded, employing people, and building a sustainable presence in a town.

The practice of sharing resources and finances in a kingdom ecosystem is like the workings of a mycorrhizal fungi network in actual living soil. Hidden underground by threads invisible to the naked eye, mycorrhizal fungi interconnect and facilitate a silent exchange of essential nutrients between plants. Often, we think that plants are competing for nutrients and resources, but in reality, through this network of connections, the living soil transports (shares) vital nutrients such as water and minerals, so that both the fungi and the plants benefit.[2]

In a kingdom economy, people get paid for work, plain and simple, but they also give their spiritual gifts in a free exchange to benefit the entire community. Everyone tries to be as little of a burden on the community purse as possible so that the growth of the ecosystem can take first place. Stay tuned for more on this in the next act.

Intentional Homes

In every kind of ecosystem, *intentional* homes of mission are important. If you just have businesses and even a great apostolic convergent space, your ecosystem will limp along unless a good majority of your people also make their actual neighborhood a mission.

The microchurch movement is a great pivot away from the existing Sunday-centric world many of us have come from, but we have to make sure that microchurches aren't just mini versions of traditional church or small groups with more missional names. The important nuance of an intentional home is that its inhabitants exhibit a sustainable and natural rhythm of life—including meals, downtime, working time, and playtime—and have a winsome, beautiful draw for those nearby. In the Halter home, we've always used the euphemism that our home is like Grand Central Station. That means that when we are home, so are a lot of others. Christmas, Thanksgiving, summer break for college students, and just about every other normal holiday means the Halter home will be full of thirty to forty people. In between those big gatherings are hundreds of days and nights when our home is the home of wayward adolescents.

When the McCalls moved to Alton, their neighborhood began to change within twelve months. In their home, fatherless kids found meals and family life they'd never known before. Eventually, those with limited access to life's essentials found open doors through this one home in a busted-up area of our town. Interestingly, we recently had a conversation with a long-time Alton resident, who told us the area where the McCall home is located seems to be returning to what it was long ago, when it had a sense of family, a more flourishing economy, and a general sense of hope.

As we look at brave cities around the country, the leaders never drive to their ecosystem. They live in it. Because they reside there, they know what their neighborhood needs—because their own kids have the same needs. They don't have to do demographic studies because they know everyone and experience similar issues. If the neighborhood is not lit well, or there are no speed bumps to stop speeding cars, they, like all their neighbors, share the stories of being underserved and having their kids almost run down. So, they work on the stuff that isn't right or good. Living intentionally in a city therefore changes a city. When we (the McCalls) first lived in Birmingham, we would always go visit our friends who lived in the marginalized areas of our city. We loved them and showed love to them. But the reality is, their problems weren't our problems. We got to leave and go back to our nice clean environment. But the incarnation of Jesus started to change my heart and mind. Jesus made my problems his problems. He faced everything I face. And eventually, we knew that we had to actually experience the weight of the community we wanted to reach, and the only way to know and feel that was to live there.

Besides the businesses, justice works, nonprofits, and whatever else is created, you simply can't get away from the need to establish incarnationally focused homes in neighborhoods. Some ecosystems prioritize buying homes in underserved neighborhoods, and in other ecosystems, they just focus on the homes they already have. Both are good and needed. Homes are where everything happens: meals, conversations, parties, casual sabbath time, work, crisis management, life mentorship, foster care, and neighborhood renewal. Just as we view extra money as something to be shared, so we can also say extra rooms, extra seats at the table, and a little extra margin are to be shared with the lonely and lost. Whether you are looking at microchurches, missional communities, or whatever you call them, make intentional homes a priority and a baseline ingredient of any kingdom ecosystem. This not only allows participation for those not involved in the business side of the ecosystem, but it also forms the seedbed of "church" as the ecosystem forms.

Tables

Bill is a guy who came into Post Commons almost every day for several years. Most of the time, he was working remotely on his laptop and would stay at least three to four hours. Bill wasn't a believer, but I (Hugh) always made sure to say hi, give a good handshake, or ask how his day was going. Bill also connected with Kristin, a woman in our community who helped lead a warming center that gives the homeless a place to find shelter during cold weather. Over time, Kristin discovered Bill had a genuine interest in helping at the warming center, and a few months later, Bill was coaching a young homeless man in our coffee shop.

As I always do whenever I go to Post Commons, I walk through and wave to our regulars. One particular day, I caught Bill's eye, and he hopped up out of his chair, much more excited than usual. I needed to use the restroom, but he seemed bent on having a conversation, so I said, "Bill, I'll find you on my way out of here." He didn't catch the hint and followed me into the lounge. I was undeterred and headed to the urinal, but Bill was right there, awkwardly over my left shoulder. "So, Bill, what's on your mind?" I asked. Excitedly he said, "Man, working with Kristin and these homeless folks has been so great. I feel like I've found my calling. I'm actually really good with them, and I feel I have a way to communicate and help them move forward." I replied, "Bill, man, I love that you have found a sense of calling by just being in this space and becoming a part of our family." With that, we parted, but I remember being so at peace with how Bill found us because the ecosystem offered him a place to drink coffee and meet new friends. Without trying, he ran into our people as they were on mission and inadvertently found his calling. This is the power of seeing our businesses and social connections as more than just a place to connect. Tables, as they were in Scripture, were where people met God and met God's friends. When Jesus taught about the culminated kingdom, he gave us a picture of a table where you'd want to run deep into the hills to find friends to invite (Matthew 22:1–10). When Jesus was physically on the earth, he constantly met with people over the table with food and conversation, and transformation happened naturally. In brave cities, we don't just build businesses. We are hoping that God will meet with us and those who hang around us as we create spaces of belonging so that people can find what they're looking for. Tables are where people get to enjoy the fruit of the harvest.

STEWARDS, WORKERS, AND SEEKERS

Whereas the church in our time has created categories of believers, atheists, pagans, sinners, unchurched, dechurched, religious, members, attenders, affirming, and non-affirming, we are presenting a new framework where we only focus on *stewards*, *workers*, and *seekers*.

Stewards are those who get an idea and make it their own, taking responsibility to establish and grow the work. They are the pioneers and foundation layers. They end up being the ones who model and set culture and who initiate and form the working team.

Workers are those who join in and grow into ownership of the ecosystem. They may not initially have as much passion for the work—or even understand what they've joined—but they experience and grow in all elements of discipleship and eventually help lead in the kingdom ecosystem. In the end, they become integral in building the tables where people find God. They are the employees, the ones who serve, the big brothers and big sisters, and most likely the ones who become the next generation of stewards. Whereas most stewards will be believers, workers don't have to be. They just have to love the work. Stewards set culture, but workers have to at least carry the culture, or you will have the natural struggle of dealing with competing or counter cultures to the one you desire to bring to the city.

Seekers are simply all the people who find themselves at our tables. They usually have no idea what we are up to or what they are joining, but they seem to find hope for whatever they are looking for and, in time, find themselves dreaming of how and what it would look like to participate and partner with us. Over time, they also tend to be drawn toward God. They are like Bill, who found his calling; or Kevin, who, over the course of twelve months, heard the story of Jesus while talking to David at the espresso machine; or Mal and Seth who helped us with events and kept asking to be invited into our spiritual times. Every story of hundreds of seekers in each of these brave cities is a natural story of someone finding what we offer, becoming curious about the spirit and authenticity of our people, and eventually finding the story of God.

NUANCES

The five architectural elements of disciples, convergent spaces, a kingdom economy, intentional homes, and tables can serve as a framework to soften and bring life to the hard, dead soil in a city. But next, we want to talk about the nuances that quite literally make all the difference in keeping the soil rich and healthy.

Incubation and Innovation

If there was an initial strategy for any brave city, it might include "incubation and innovation"—the processes whereby new and fresh ideas are formed and implemented. From the very beginning, we need to ask questions such as "How do we bring hope and life to this neighborhood?" "What business would be helpful and add value in this context?" or "What mission would be most effective in exposing the kingdom to these people?" When incubation and innovation are central to the ecosystem, new works are regularly being empowered and released. A culture of dreaming and risk becomes normal, and the citizens begin to live in the reality that they can do anything they feel called to. All spaces become sacred. All laity become priests in their own right.

During the pandemic, one brave city doubled its businesses. How? Because the struggle of the pandemic forced creativity and released a lot of free time as people were not gathering publicly, so they had the capacity to build new businesses. Pain and struggle, although not enjoyable, are actually helpful in this phase and provide clues as to how new work addresses immediate needs. The old adage, "necessity is the mother of invention," is true.

Anonymity and Humility

If you were to give people the option to eat mass-produced food versus food from a local farm-to-table co-op, most people would probably choose to buy and eat from what seems like a smaller, more family-owned establishment. In reality, though, almost everything we eat is from a farm. It's just that some farms are massive and owned by huge marketing companies, and some are small and unknown. Still, the perception of how our food is produced is important. Right now, many people mistrust anything mass-produced, manipulated, or backed by "big money." That applies to large food conglomerates that might claim something is "heart healthy" or a megachurch that has some campaign to "love our city." Trust is hard to gain now, and so the posture by which we do the works is as important as the actual works themselves.

In Matthew 6:3–4, Jesus asked us to give and not let our right hand know what the left hand was doing. This point gets missed by those of us who feel it is our responsibility to go out in public and "reach the lost," but in saying this, Jesus was trying to help us build credibility. Yes, I know, we were given T-shirts that clearly show our church name and its vision statement, and we were always taught that anytime we are nice, hand out water bottles, or do a good deed, we should make sure the recipients know who did this for them. But Jesus knows we err any time we promote our own good works. He also knows how powerful it is when we do consistent good works without ever talking about them … at all. Jesus never talked about himself. He let others talk about him. He'd heal people and then tell them not to say anything. We believe that the desire of brave cities to be anonymous is actually what allows them to shine and gives real credibility to the story of Jesus. As people of God, we are to be people without guile or selfish motivations for why and what we do for others. If we recognize God's favor on something we do, we celebrate it among ourselves.

Decentralization and Distributed Structures

Decentralization is defined as the transfer of control of an activity or an organization from the few to the many. For centuries, the form, functions, priesthood, and polity of the church have been centralized around a few people or in one place. We've got to flip this model on its head. Both place and people need to be spread throughout an area or an ecosystem. Leadership should happen from the bottom rather than the top and be circular rather than hierarchical. And the most gifted leaders and the most magnetic spaces must look to empower others and expand outward. As we decentralize, kingdom movements become less and less dependent on single leaders or single visions. What becomes natural is a culture of going out as opposed to inviting in; a culture of innovation instead of stagnation; a culture of interconnected creative works instead of franchised carbon copies; a culture of adversity and risk instead of safety and security. It's virtually impossible to stop a decentralized movement. The target is constantly moving to the point where there is no target. In its purest form, the church is a decentralized yet interconnected ecosystem where all parts are working together in a city or context to create tables of hope.

Practically, the values of decentralization and distribution come from the theology that Jesus only has one church. Really, only one. Thus, we never feel the pressure to get everyone to play in our gardens. We just want to throw seeds everywhere and help others create. There's never any competition, coercion, pressure, or judgment for people who may not fully find their identity with us. We really don't care, as long as they are growing, working, and deepening their own faith and missional expression. Jesus and his mission must be the identity and brand we push instead of our own organizational brand.

In one brave city, a young African-American leader with a great vision didn't feel comfortable organizing or carrying out her work under the white leader who had pioneered the ecosystem. Although it was explained that the white leader was more of a father in the movement and had no literal control over her mission, it didn't matter. The pain of her experience from past white leaders was too acute, and she chose to pursue her work without the formal link to the ecosystem. But the white leader and his entire ecosystem continued to love, serve, pray, and financially support this woman's work. Why? Because of the ecosystem that God is building in that town. In other words, a city ecosystem is a part of God's larger ecosystem. Yes, things move more easily and generally last longer the more people trust each other, but we love to see brave cities helping build God's ecosystem that may include other good works that "play alongside" or "partner with" instead of being "in covenant with" or being "formally connected to."

Access

Our city, like many impoverished areas, is considered a "food desert." A food desert is a place where people have limited access to affordable or nutritious food. Every time I (Hugh) drive to the grocery store, there is a line of people waiting to carry their one or two grocery bags onto a municipal bus to take them back home. They have to plan out their day just to figure out how to get one or two miles to where decent food is. Because of the hassle, many just opt for the chips or chicken nuggets they can get at the local gas station. Overcoming food deserts requires lots of small local farms or local community gardens to grow great fresh produce.

Small local farms can be difficult to establish and maintain, but we must do what we can to help people get access to fresh food grown in living soil.

So, when you think of alleviating poverty, just think of helping people access what you have. That might mean working to meet physical needs such as food and housing, felt needs such as community and family, emotional needs such as spaces to process pain and provide healing, or spiritual needs such as the hope of life and purpose in Jesus. On a relational level, those in poverty often struggle to rise above their circumstances, simply because they don't have any big brothers or sisters, moms and dads, or grandparents to impart wisdom and help them find their way. In the same way, the clearest understanding of "good news" is access to all of these things. Brave cities create geographical and relational access. We move into neighborhoods simply to offer the stability of our family, our food, and our presence. We start businesses in the parts of town that need the most renewal. When we start a youth basketball team, we buy uniforms, shoes, and socks if needed; we pay the league dues and provide transportation to every single practice or game because if we can't give them access to all the things they need, it's not worth starting the work in the first place.

Togetherness and Proximity

Something notable and mysterious happens when kingdom people encounter other kingdom people: faith, hope, and love are transferred in a tangible and recognizable way. The idea of not forsaking the assembling of ourselves together and stirring up one another to love and good works (Hebrews 10:24–25) was meant to be far more robust and holistic than sitting in rows one day a week and listening to a lecture. The call to consistent gatherings must be something far beyond a worship event. Though meetings of kingdom people need not be advertised, and indeed we prefer a low-key approach, the context in the first century was that God's people shouldn't hide out alone in their homes for fear of religious persecution. The call to gather was a call to visible witness, communal mission, prayer, and to be a signpost of the kingdom. These convergent spaces were often out in the open or in a known spot.

Today, these convergent spaces could be intentional homes, businesses, or social spaces where people know they will encounter other people filled with kingdom hope—as we carry the power and presence of God. When a young Black businesswoman died in our area, suddenly leaving behind three kids and our only Black-owned downtown business, it crushed our city with sadness. People were Facebooking their love, putting flowers out at her business, and more than $100,000 was raised within a week to help transport her body back from Jamaica and pay for all the funeral expenses. Post Commons is the largest gathering space in town, so we simply offered to host the reception right after her memorial service. Our brave city mobilized, donated the space and all the drinks, and served to make it a great evening. And all that night, I kept thinking, *Don't forsake the gathering together of the saints.* We gathered to serve instead of being served. We gathered to encourage instead of to be encouraged. We gathered to give money instead of collecting money. Our proximity and togetherness aren't about facilitating church; they support our ability to react and bless in the daily life experiences in our city that call for action.

Levity and Suffering

Within our small community in Alton we have a lot of toddlers, and because we're always together, we are often all sick at the same time. Most of our folks, as a rule of life, have chosen to take on challenging activities. We have foster parents, firefighters, high school teachers, as well as those who work with the homeless and care for addicts. That means every week someone is suffering or has seen a lot of suffering. Lack of sleep, lack of resources, and the occasional tragedy seem to always be lurking around the corner.

In the last three years, the Halter family lost their son, Ryan, and then almost lost their youngest daughter, McKenna, after she miscarried her baby and nearly bled out. Hugh called me (Taylor) one day when he thought McKenna was not going to make it and shared that he was standing in the middle of his driveway having a complete physical and emotional breakdown. He said, "I … I just shit my pants … literally." Knowing Hugh didn't need a lecture on self-care or Bible verses to encourage him, I just said, "Maybe it would be a good time to go hose yourself down." Hugh told me later, it was that simple tone of humor that got him through one of the worst moments of his adult life.

Though this is an extreme example, it illustrates a unique attribute of our community that has played out in hundreds of tough moments. Our ability to face difficulty with composure, humor, and grace has become a hallmark and a primary witness of our community in the city. People commented on how well our businesses handled the struggle of COVID-19, or how well the Halters handled death, or how the McCalls handled fatherless kids, or how another family—the Piocos—handled a challenging foster care lifestyle. Levity while in the midst of severe trials speaks volumes.

If there's anything that marks our cultural moment, it is angst and passion. This intensity forms the undercurrent that creates division, hatred, racism, whacky patriotism, rage, and violence. Jesus said, "By this everyone will know that you are my disciples, if you love one another" (John 13:35). He didn't say this to a homogenous, white-gated country club community; he said it to a world that was already full of division. He was asking his disciples to be unlike the rest of the world of haters, race baiters, gay bashers, critics, deconstructors, judgmental Pharisees, and hypocrites of all orders. He was asking that, amid all the other fighting in the world, we would choose to fight for unity and love. Personally, we've found that the secret of unity is levity; the ability not to take our own, or anyone else's, opinions or actions too seriously, including the sins they so easily fall into. Levity allows us to let God have total control over how and how fast he wants to change someone's mind, heart, or actions. We're not talking about sarcastic smirks or rolling of the eyes; we're suggesting a steadfast, peaceful, and prayerful commitment to hold space for the Spirit to work. Levity, laughter, and long-suffering set an atmosphere in which people can stay on mission and stay together for the long haul.

To summarize: A kingdom ecosystem needs unique disciples, convergent spaces, a kingdom economy, intentional homes, and tables surrounded by stewards, workers, and seekers. This ecosystem works best when planted in the rich soil of the kingdom's nuances of incubation and innovation, anonymity and humility, decentralized and distributed structures, access, togetherness and proximity, levity and suffering. Next, some more specifics.

Act Four

FREE MARKET
CHURCH

The Economy of Acts for Today

At the present time your plenty will supply what they need, so that in turn their plenty will supply what you need. The goal is equality, as it is written: "The one who gathered much did not have too much, and the one who gathered little did not have too little."
2 CORINTHIANS 8:14–15

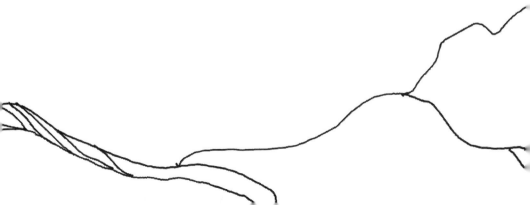

When you drive down Crenshaw Boulevard in Los Angeles, or through inner-city Birmingham or Detroit, you'll notice two things that stand in stark contrast to each other. First, there is an abundance of churches, all with wild names; and second, there is the absolute blight in the streets. World Outreach Center, Church of the King, Kingdom Revolution, The Shepherd's Gate, and Jubilee Center all have names that would cause you to think that this street or area of the city should be pretty darn close to God's vision for his new kingdom. And yet you have to literally walk over crack-addicted homeless men and women to get to them. It begs a question … the same question you eventually ask when you go to Nigeria or India, and people tell you how many millions came to a revival or how many hundreds of thousands of churches have been planted; but all you see at every level of society is corruption, greed, haves and have-nots, religious legalism and abuse, and all the other things that would exist if Satan were calling the shots. The question is, why is it like this?

In America, megachurches line the streets of the suburbs and encourage every member to take "financial peace" courses where gurus teach that tithing is the key to kingdom life and debt-free living. Yes, it is a business model, and it's a wise discipleship model if you are trying to keep people giving to a centralized system where some money goes out to the needs of the city—though in ever-decreasing amounts as the church declines.

The tithe is often taught as a spiritual discipline that will result in God's blessing. But with the massive decline in church attendance, the global pandemic, the Russian invasion of Ukraine, surging oil prices, and twenty other factors, people are holding onto whatever financial security they can. And yes, the poor—who just keep being poor—are ever-increasing.

The business model of church attendance, passing the offering plate, and calling people to give 10 percent of their income is a dying model; and it's not always been very helpful to the world. At its best, this model allows the pure in heart to express their trust in God by putting their money where their mouth is. It's impressive when you run into a Christian who has been committed to giving their entire life. But what if you can be a faithful giver *and* a more strategic giver? What if giving to a central command that spends more than 80 percent of all incoming funds on church infrastructure is the worst form of kingdom investment? Maybe faithful giving could instead look like supporting small kingdom ecosystems, where ills that plague our society are being addressed.

Friends, without micro-critiquing a typical church in America, we must acknowledge that the people of God are not being challenged to live and give sacrificially. Although "religious people" tend to give more overall than "non-religious people," much of this money often goes to local churches for maintaining pastors' salaries, church buildings, and administrative expenses. And, "less-religious" people (including atheists) tend to give more toward causes that touch their hearts—out of compassion or an emotional connection to another person or situation—while "more-religious" people have been shown to ground their generosity less in emotion and more in other factors, such as a doctrine or concerns over their reputations.[1] Clearly, we need to issue a call for greater personal discipleship in this area.

Most of Jesus' teaching on money is about the heart of the giver, not the giving of money itself. Thus, any system of collected and distributed funds, if not propelled and inspired by real needs, eventually leads to a lack of vision and faith. And Jesus clearly warned against that in Luke 16, in what we know as "the parable of the shrewd manager." This teaching wasn't a knock on the dishonesty of an unbeliever; it was a scathing rebuke of believers who aren't wise with their money. We need to see Jesus as the financier of the new economy and allow him to redefine our view of church, family, and finances. This involves moving away from the dominant, consumer-driven economy and creating a new system that operates in contrast to it. This new economy, as we will see, not only provides sustainability for the mission but reveals the gospel and God's heart for lifting people out of the muck and mire of poverty, injustice, and systemic ills. God's system of giving also deeply affects and changes the heart of every believer. For him, you cannot be a disciple if you are not living from faith, generosity, and sacrifice.

STARTING WHERE JESUS STARTED

In Luke 4:18–19, Jesus walks into a synagogue, is handed the scroll from the prophet Isaiah, and then fingers through until he finds a passage from Isaiah 61. He then stands up, preparing himself to read to the large crowd, who are curious about him. He's about to announce the beginning of his new reign. He could have chosen a hundred different scriptures that would accurately describe some elements of what his kingdom would be about, but he selects one that encapsulates the larger, more important, comprehensive story of what he wants to reveal. Reading from the scroll, he says: "The Spirit of the Lord is on me, because he has anointed me to preach good news to the poor. He has sent me to proclaim freedom for the prisoners and recovery of sight for the blind, to release the oppressed, to proclaim the year of the Lord's favor."

Then he calmly rolls up the scroll, gives it back to the attendant, and sits down. With the eyes of everyone in the synagogue fastened on him, he continues: "Today this scripture is fulfilled in your hearing" (v. 21).

Boom, mic drop, game on!

When you read all the redemptive results of the gospel alluded to in Isaiah 61, it can be perceived as a "do-gooders handbook" of justice and how the church should be active with the poor and marginalized. For sure, these elements are there, but don't miss the point of what Jesus was announcing. To say that prisoners would be set free, oppressed folk would be released, and that a specific year of the Lord's favor was taking place, would not have been a strange idea to his listeners. Every Jewish listener would have heard those words in the context of their Jewish economic and national story that the prophets constantly reminded them of—and that God, through Jesus, was now focusing on. Like a magnifying glass that takes a wide source of light and focuses it into a tight, bright, hot center that could literally start a fire, Jesus is reestablishing God's original economy of daily provision coupled with sharing so that the needs of his community are taken care of. It was a reminder of what some call a "manna economy."[2]

But Jesus' listeners missed this central point, and so do we. They had forgotten about the white-hot center of God's heart for the world and were now "generally" trying to be religious and decent. But just like we see on Crenshaw Boulevard or the inner city of Detroit, their recreational-level devoutness, their numbness, their lack of engagement had once again caused their world to descend into hoarding, coveting, stealing, violence, and every form of injustice and division you can imagine. People fought for themselves, leaving those with limited access caught in a cycle of poverty and stress, causing them to do whatever they could to make ends meet.

Jesus didn't just say, "Hey my kingdom is starting, but you can go to church with your friends every week, give your 10 percent tithe, and then get on with your individualistic, consumeristic, material-istic lifestyle." The announcement of his new kingdom signaled the inauguration of a societal and economic overhaul, not a privatized salvation opportunity. To Jesus, being "saved" meant joining his global takeover against greed, injustice, and poverty. There may be nothing wrong with tithing, but the way we do it, there may also be nothing right about it. At best it's neutral, and at worst it props up the consumer church as a spiritualized racket.

If Jesus' economy could lift people out and up, but the world's economies are fraught with greed and selfish motives, would the small works of a brave city have any impact? Would they be worth all the effort?

Here's our simple answer: The kingdom economy is not going to completely change and replace the world's economy, but the economy of a brave city sustains that individual community and its mission. Over time that will have a ripple effect, demonstrating to those watching that something different and good is afoot. A brave city is actually and tangibly a city of refuge—operated on an economy where everyone has an opportunity to work and an invitation to a meal, a family, and a great conversation about the King. It can be small or large; the size and the impact aren't actually the point. The more important thing is whether it's based on the things Jesus read from Isaiah 61. Is there good news for the poor? Is there liberty for the captives? Is the Lord's favor here?

A small nonprofit that is part of Lantern Network in Alton has just raised $100,000 to install the first soccer mini-pitch in the greater St. Louis area. That may not seem like kingdom work, but our town has barely any public spaces for kids, and there are very few athletic programs. Damian, who started this effort, has a love for kids, a love for the underprivileged, and a love and deep connection with the brand-new professional soccer team in St. Louis. He knows and prophetically sees how this one little investment will create a web of kingdom life for our community, and how it will make a discernible difference. Whether we're transforming a boarded-up building into a community center, or creating a coffee shop, soccer field, or intentional neighborhood home, the city feels the impact as soon as the funds are allocated. The Crenshaw Boulevards in our country need real help; and the economy of a brave city delivers, even if the investment starts as small as a seed.

MODERN-DAY MANNA: THE ECONOMY OF THE DESERT WANDERERS

In Exodus 16, when the Israelites, wandering the wilderness, started grumbling about not having enough food, God responded by promising to "rain down bread from heaven" (v. 4). When that bread appeared, it took the form of thin, frostlike flakes. Looking at that "bread," the bewildered people uttered a Hebrew word, *manhue*, which means "what is it?" (That's the word we know today as "manna.") Imagine being promised bread and instead learning that you are going to be eating some weird substance you find lying on the ground every morning. What's more, God is telling you to gather only what you need for the day, and not to hoard any more or it will rot the next day … but, trust him, there will be more the next morning. It would be as ludicrous to us today as it was for them back then. God was asking his people to surrender control, planning, and foresight and to get used to living as missionaries, trusting God every day for supernatural provision.

Manna taught the Israelites to trust in God's ability to meet their needs and introduced them to an economy of equity. Exodus 16:18 says that some gathered much, and some gathered little, but when they brought the manna back and measured it, everyone had just as much as they needed. It's what Paul talked about when he said in 2 Corinthians 9:8–12,

> And God is able to bless you abundantly, so that in all things at all times, having all that you need, you will abound in every good work. As it is written: "They have freely scattered their gifts to the poor; their righteousness endures forever." Now he who supplies seed to the sower and bread for food will also supply and increase your store of seed and will enlarge the harvest of your righteousness. You will be enriched in every way so that you can be generous on every occasion, and through us your generosity will result in thanksgiving to God. This service that you perform is not only supplying the needs of the Lord's people but is also overflowing in many expressions of thanks to God.

Manna economics is what the book of Acts and every subsequent faithful community operates from. It's a communal and relational practice that connects us to Jesus and anchors us to our daily mission and faith in the God who sends us. God's economy isn't just for us; it's for the world he is serving through us.

Interestingly, the manna economy was essential to the spiritual and communal rhythm of Sabbath, of resting with the community for a day in remembrance of God's guidance and provision of a desert people. God only allowed the Israelites to collect enough manna for each day or it would spoil, except for the day before the Sabbath. On the day before the Sabbath, they could gather twice as much manna, and it did not rot on the day of rest. Those who tried to collect manna on the Sabbath found nothing on the ground that day.

In Deuteronomy 8:2–4, Moses reminds the Israelites of God's guidance and provision in the desert. Quoting Moses's words, Jesus rebuffs Satan's efforts to tempt him in the desert by telling him that "It takes more than bread to stay alive" (Matthew 4:4 MSG). Jesus is saying there is another kind of sustenance for us all.

Reinforcing our reorientation to the manna economy, theologian Ched Myers reminds us,

> The Hebrew bible's vision of the Sabbath economics contends that the theology of abundant grace and a communal ethic of redistribution is the only way out of our slavery to the debt system, with its theology of meritocracy and private ethic of wealth concentration. The contemporary church, however, has difficulty hearing this as good news since our theological imaginations have long been captive to the market-driven orthodoxies of modern capitalism.[3]

That is to say, if you use financial guru Dave Ramsey as your Moses so that you can become a millionaire completely free from debt, *but* you miss the opportunities of communal mission, risk, and the covenant of sharing while avoiding Jesus' warnings not to store up treasures (Matthew 6:19–21), then you've still missed his supernatural economy. Didn't Jesus call the rich young ruler to sell his stuff and give it to the poor (Matthew 19:16–30)? Why? Maybe because it isn't good for the rich man or woman to be completely without need or dependence upon the community. Did you catch that? If you always find yourself being the one who's giving but never needing, that could be a big problem. It is possible that the difficulty a rich man or woman might have in accessing the life of the kingdom is simply but profoundly because their wealth tells them they don't need anyone.

When Rodney left his paid pastoral position to start Soulcraft—a woodworking mentoring process for young men and women—it cost him a salary, and he also had to pay out of his own pocket for retail and workers' spaces, plus equipment and tools. He aims to do enough paid commissioned furniture work to help subsidize all he gives to these young folks. Sometimes that income covers his expenses, and sometimes he adds other odd jobs to make it work. Within our network, we all live week-to-week or month-to-month, and often we alert each other to earning opportunities that might help us get by. We all hustle, we all share our needs, and we all help each other. It's tempting to think it would be easier to have millions to give away, but this can be a trap, and living by the manna economy as part of a community is much more fulfilling.

Said more fundamentally, God gives us everything we need, and more, every day; and then asks us to live a life of sharing. Those who want to claim allegiance to Jesus but control and keep everything they think they've made by themselves and for themselves must be reading a different Bible.

Now, hearing all of this, you may, like us, say, "Well, that's just too hard. No one would really do that church-of-Acts thing where you sell land, houses, and cars, liquidate your Bitcoin account, and then only keep what you need." And of course, most of us would also point out that we've got to put away money for retirement in case we live into our mid-90s—which the people in the early church didn't have to worry about. For sure, we do live in a different day and age … but we have to ask again, what would happen to the street credibility of our Christian movement and the collective witness of the church if we actually tried this? We all know the answer—it would be amazing! It would require us to live as the church, instead of recreationally going to a church service and then returning to our normal lives. It would force us into a day-to-day community that must think together, pray together, work together, and do whatever is necessary to keep the mission moving.

Here's an idea: Just start with your table. My (Taylor's) wife, Lindsey, says all the time, "There are no hungry people at our table." We can't change the whole world, but we can end loneliness, hunger, and fatherlessness tonight at our table. See what grows from there.

LET THE PROPHETS SPEAK AGAIN!

Throughout time, God's people have always resisted his kingdom economics, so in the Old Testament, he had to keep sending people to speak for him. Hosea 2:5 calls out the Israelites for putting their hope in foreign sources instead of God's "manna." Jeremiah 34:13–16 hammers the Israelites for going back on their commitment to the every-seven-year Jubilee, where prisoners and slaves were set free (see Leviticus 25). Nehemiah 5:6–13 challenges the nobles and officials of the day to stop charging "usury" (exorbitant interest) that further held people down. In Isaiah 3:14–15, the prophet railed against the rich for stealing from and exploiting the poor.

When Jesus came, he was calling his followers back to what Moses and the prophets were trying to accomplish: convincing God's people to live by manna economics, kingdom jubilee, justice, redistribution, and radical sharing. As a result, the early church community operated in such a way that "there were no needy persons among them" (Acts 4:34). They understood that the primary message of the gospel was that a new kingdom had been made available, and that the good news of the kingdom of God is freedom for those held captive by poverty, sickness, inequity, or sin. Today, we often think of the death and resurrection of Jesus as the whole message of the gospel; but the gospel is more than that.

The good news didn't start and stop with his life, death, and resurrection. He was the one who made the gospel of a new kingdom available! This might run counter to what many of us have been taught, but Jesus himself went through Galilee "proclaiming the good news of the kingdom, and healing every disease and sickness among the people" (Matthew 4:23). What gospel or "good news" was Jesus proclaiming if he hadn't yet died and been resurrected? The early church understood this in a way that Christians today have failed to grasp.

A flash-fire movement and societal change happened because the Jesus-community became known as people who took care of people. Where the Israelites failed, the church was to model a new economy of sharing, removing debt, and working hard so as not to be a burden.

They were making a difference to the world around them, and in doing so, they were pointing people to Jesus. Today, if you tell people how many converts you made or how many baptisms or decisions you saw, most people don't care. And most young people we talk with today are completely skeptical of those who only mentally assent to Christianity without actually being converted to the way of Jesus. There is an expectation that if someone follows Jesus, they will also take on the economic priorities of Jesus, just as they would take on any other aspect of his life. They see the Crenshaw Boulevards and the struggling single moms with no hope who live next door and say "bullshit" to the churches, as well as to leaders on both sides of our American government, who say they want to help but have no real connection to the needs of those we actually love. The giver seeking to seriously follow Jesus wants to make a true kingdom investment.

In response to all of this, we wonder whether church planting is really what God wants if it doesn't establish a new communal economic option for people that blesses the cities we live in. Is it better to plant small brave cities than plant large consumer churches? It might be.

MODERN-DAY ANANIAS AND SAPPHIRA

Probably the strangest and most off-putting story in the New Testament is found in Acts 5:1–15. People in the "manna community" were sharing their stuff so generously that it was making crazy headlines in their town. One couple, Ananias and Sapphira, after claiming to have given all the proceeds from the sale of some property, decided to keep some of it for themselves. Both of them instantly died, and the news spread throughout both the believing and the unbelieving (or trying to believe) community. If you're like us, you read this and are like … *what?*

God was letting them (and us) know that the issue of money is serious to him. A key concept of portraying God's true nature and the gospel to an onlooking world is through a sort of "communal jubilee"—letting people off the hook, providing for them even if they get themselves in a jam, and taking care of people's practical needs. This gracious attitude sets people free. It brings Jesus into the rooms of community halls, local coffee shops, and makerspaces, and releases the aroma of freedom.

Who wouldn't want that? Can you think of any poor or marginalized people who wouldn't love this gospel? But some don't like it—those of us who want to appear to be gospel people but still keep a tight grip on all our stuff. As Luke 1:53 prophetically told, there will be many who are at odds with this gospel because "he has filled the hungry with good things, but has sent the rich away empty."

Jesus leveled his harshest judgments at the religious leaders who used the gospel for personal gain. One of Jesus' best friends sold him out for a year's wages and foreshadowed the struggle all ministers potentially face when trying to earn a living from their work with Jesus. Perhaps Judas was the most trustworthy of the disciples since he was given the responsibility of holding the funds for everyone. He was certainly present during some of the most intimate and powerful moments with Jesus. It's safe to assume he, like all the others, loved Jesus and started his journey thankful to be one of Jesus' disciples.

But—whatever his complicated motivations—in one powerful moment Judas took the opportunity to profit from his relationship with Jesus. It was his "kiss of death" and signals the peril for others who trade the call of God for financial security.

When Jesus met with Levi, the tax collector, he wasn't just concerned with Levi's afterlife (Mark 2:13–14). He was offering him freedom from a corrupt economy and calling him to the liberty of kingdom finances. When Jesus associated with prostitutes (see Luke 7:36–50), he was creating a community that cared for and included these women as sisters, so they would no longer have to sell their bodies for money. By challenging the rich rulers to give away all their wealth (as in Matthew 19:16–30), Jesus understood that a new economy was just as crucial to their conversion as a renewed heart. Many of Jesus' parables relate to money or to economic concerns, so we must have ears to hear how following Jesus impacts our approach to money and how our business ventures and places of business may be the new evangelism or "good news" for the church.

A COFFEE SHOP WON'T FIX EVERYTHING

We're taking some time on the spiritual side of economy because often when people visit our kingdom ecosystems, they can be wowed by the cool coffee shops, makerspaces, or edgy justice works and fall in love with the "vibe." But we always remind people, unless you are building an alternative spiritual community, all the enterprise can fall far short, and you'd be doing yourself a favor by just *going* to a coffee shop instead of *building* one. Jesus challenged potential disciples to count the cost; not just the cost of a building for the business, but the cost of understanding what God is building, your motivations with money, and how much it will cost you to live according to kingdom economics.

Besides Jesus' kingdom economy being the evangelistic playing field, it is also essential in discipleship. Our growth must involve trusting in God to provide our manna, as well as trusting him to supernaturally impact our world rather than doing everything in our own strength. When Jesus called his disciples, he was asking them to turn their back on mammon—the money of the Romans—and any currency that pulled them away from kingdom life. If you analyze Jesus' parables, you'll see just how much he connects discipleship with our mindset and management of our financial resources. Jesus talks about trusting God for provision, giving generously with joy, and the choice of serving either God or money.

The community of Jesus is a body, and there's no part of the body that is more important than the other; and there's no need for comparison or categories of intelligence, class, or wealth. Jesus' discipleship is a call to daily jubilee. In other words, we look to help our brothers and sisters stabilize, contribute, invest, risk, and grow their portfolios on behalf of the body. Instead of the majority of the church's resources going to a few religious leaders and church buildings, Jesus' economy is about empowerment, justice, and becoming last so that others can be first (Matthew 19:30). We have heard this phrase forever, but until you see it in the original context of economics, you won't be set free or make whole disciples.

Again, evangelism and discipleship are not just about conversion but are also invitations to tables with Jesus—tables that the community or body creates for those who have been held out or held down from participation. The tables in our homes and businesses are where justice and inclusion are seen and experienced. In Luke 14:7–14, Jesus tells us to invite the poor and outcast to our parties and to take the lowest place at the table, challenging the social hierarchies that produce the ladder-climbing, coveting, and privatizing of faith that destroy evangelistic opportunities. To Jesus, when you create a body of friends who share their time, their money, and their tables and no longer see people from a worldly point of view, then you have created reconciled spaces, where people can share a table, food, and life together.

BUSINESS IS NOT *FOR* OR *AS* MISSION ... BUSINESS *IS* THE MISSION

Do you remember the days of Christian Yellow Pages? The world had the big fat Yellow Pages with all the businesses in town, and then we had our itsy bitsy little Christian Yellow Pages that we all assumed we should consult first. A common belief in that day was that if you were a Christian, then your business was Christian too. Christian businesses were thought to be a Christian witness and "on mission" simply because they had the fish symbol at the bottom of their ads and business cards. There's nothing inherently wrong in this, but all our Christian businesses and brands didn't really impress anyone or make any tangible difference. Often, in fact, they repelled the culture either by doing substandard work or by not offering services to those in the pagan community (like refusing to bake cakes for their gay weddings).

In a kingdom economy, the businesses are not *for* mission; they *are* the mission. Offering good food, good coffee, beautiful landscaping, useful products, inviting spaces, family environments ... these are all forms of good news. It's holistic evangelism. What are the stories we want to tell? That someone found Jesus while doing CrossFit, or having a beer, or while sweating their tails off building an outdoor patio in the middle of the summer. When the business becomes the mission, things change. It's no longer "Buy our Christian coffee to support our mission"; now it's, "Buy our coffee because it's good coffee, and because we want to know your name, hear your story, tell you ours, and maybe just maybe sniff a whiff of the redeeming work of Jesus together in everyday life ... and not require you to wear specific clothing, say specific words, or join specific groups."

When business is simply a table in the overarching city-building mission, you're free to curate something beautiful; to tell the good news of Jesus and the kingdom through a creative venture, to take a risk, and to make disciples in the everyday work of your hands.

We don't have to separate our work and our ministry anymore. No more boxes. No more compartmentalization.

You might recall that one of President Trump's big goals was to see the stock market hit 30,000 points. It was a special number to him, and when he achieved it, he bragged about it and attributed it to his own leadership.[4] He clearly grew up in the school of Milton Friedman. Most economists know that name, as Friedman penned a famous article that essentially said the sole purpose of business is to make a profit for shareholders.[5] On face value, it makes sense, but it has led to massive abuses of payouts, backhanded deals, government interference, and greed.

Interestingly, in 2020 there was a business roundtable hosted by Larry Fink of the American multinational investment company BlackRock. At that roundtable, in opposition to the Friedman doctrine, the company emphasized the importance of a company's public purpose and a commitment to "serve all stakeholders including employees, customers, supply chain, communities where we operate, and shareholders."[6] That meeting signaled a fundamental shift in the world of business and finance.[7] A new economy of conscientious profit was born. Sure, there are still plenty of businesses operating by the Friedman way, and follow-through has sometimes been difficult, but there are enterprises that prioritize the values of sustainability, creativity, freedom, gig economy, lack of debt and overwork, and benevolence that undergird this new secular economy in America. The business world is leading the way; the church should at least jump in and show some love and commitment to the common good.

Currently, the church in its institutional, Sunday-centric, pastor-centric, consumer-centric form is the poorest form of business we can think of. If any other business had as its only goal to survive and keep paying the owner while offering a shoddy product that hardly anyone is drawn to, we would tell those business owners to get out of town. And so does God. This part of our challenge is probably the one that feels hardest to accept, but we can't minimize it just because it seems hard or because so few Christians live this way. We wouldn't dismiss the clear teaching of the Sermon on the Mount simply because we know very few Christians live by the radical ethic of loving enemies and so forth. In the same way, we can't ignore Jesus' clear teaching on money. We cannot build kingdom ecosystems without letting the economy of the kingdom be the framework we are discipling into the community.

THE KINGDOM IS NOT ABOUT CHARITY

This new economy offers the potential to end pure charity or putting Band-Aids on societal ills. Kingdom economics are driven by a continual call to help people become self-sustaining and eventually a part of the kingdom-sharing model. Whereas charity is often more about making ourselves feel better, justice-based Jesus-economics is about finding out what belongs to whom and giving it back to them. The kingdom is about freedom and dignity, and it doesn't succeed when we just get someone through a rough patch, but they end up back where they started. This also applies to the nonprofits that simply solicit money instead of looking for ways to build sustainability for support. In contrast, some nonprofits are now getting in on the investment game, acquiring properties and building businesses to offset operating costs. Some churches are selling underused properties and reallocating funds into business development. We see some pastors redirecting their church salaries into building small businesses that support their calling.

Thankfully, in many spheres, temporary charity efforts are fading away, and instead, self-sustaining communities of freedom are growing. Whenever possible, we should try to avoid using funds merely to keep something or someone going. Instead, we should use money as investment capital—as "seed money." We may lose money on some investments, but seed gifts are designed to help someone, or something, become sustainable or at least partially sustainable. And if you are someone who receives such funds, we advise you not to request additional financial resources that aren't designated as "seed money," so that you can gradually ask for less and less support over time. You may have people who continue to fund your mission, but their ongoing support should be for expanding the ecosystem instead of just propping up the original investment.

As we try to outline church as a city within a city, the marketplace must become central again to the life and mission of the church. No, we are not saying that Christians should be good Christian businesspeople or that businesses are a part of God's mission. We are again saying that business *was* and *is* the mission!

AN ECONOMY FOR EVERYONE

Almost every person from a non-white ethnicity has had to work other part-time or full-time jobs in order to plant churches. I (Hugh) have been on the church-speaking circuit for many years, and I address mainly white and suburban people. The wealth within these circles has paid for leaders to receive training, attend seminary, raise donor funds for personal support, and earn large salaries at large churches.

But you don't have the same privilege if you're Somali, Burmese, Native American, African American, Hispanic, or one of the hundreds of other non-white ethnicities—or if you're following Jesus away from the suburbs into inner-city, under-resourced neighborhoods. In these sacred spaces, you cannot raise support, your churches won't grow large, and you won't be able to receive enough resources from those you're ministering to. Continually relying on outside donor support just doesn't work, and this financial model is finally failing, even in the 'burbs.

So, an economy based on enterprise was, is, and will be your best play to stay true and make it in your context. And although it's hard, it is at least doable as has been repeatedly proved by immigrant and refugee communities that relocated and built their own economies.

Look at the Bosnian community in south city St. Louis, the Hmong community on the east side of Portland, or the Indian community or any of the other immigrant communities that struggled but eventually thrived after they got off Ellis Island in New York, and you'll find people who had nothing but built everything (including church) for their people.

THE NEW TRAPPIST ORDERS

When folks ask what we're doing in Alton or what these other kingdom ecosystems are, we say, they are sort of like "new Trappist orders." St. Benedict, in the sixth century, set up the Benedictine order with the motto, *ora et labora* (literally "pray and work"), which led them to see prayer as work and work as prayer. As we've said, this phrase is the motto of our work in Alton, and it is etched throughout our Post Commons building. It encapsulates important concepts that undergird all we do. The Trappists (who came out of the Cistercian monastery of La Trappe, France) followed the Rule of St. Benedict. They were the only monastic order that didn't beg for money. Instead, they earned it, in part by brewing beer.[8] It seems they asked the question all good missionaries ask: "What would be good news here?" Because the water was often not clean, their beer met a local need while funding their charitable work.

Similarly, Paul didn't depend on others for personal support. He saw work as a central witness to God's kingdom and pointed out that it allowed him to avoid being a burden to the community. Working kept him from being dependent or enslaved and was a means to bless others.

> For you yourselves know how you ought to follow our example. We were not idle when we were with you, nor did we eat anyone's food without paying for it. On the contrary, we worked night and day, laboring and toiling so that we would not be a burden to any of you. We did this, not because we do not have the right to such

help, but in order to offer ourselves as a model for you to imitate. For even when we were with you, we gave you this rule: "The one who is unwilling to work shall not eat."

2 THESSALONIANS 3:7–10

Part of the culture in New Testament times was the practice of slavery or indentured servitude.[9] Many also owed taxes to the religious leaders and the Romans, so everyone was taking a cut out of their hard work. You can imagine the burden and the corruption associated with this system of debt and payment. Many were cheating and stealing. Many were begging for food or begging for a new husband to care for their needs. And of course, many would offer sexual favors as currency. People had very little freedom, and the idea of work rarely felt positive or hopeful. But Paul modeled an example of work redeemed from the original curse, bringing blessing rather than burden. Similarly, work in a brave city is about bringing back the freedom, the ownership, the partnership, and the blessing of work as it was intended to be.

In a brave city, work is part of becoming freer and freeing others up. In the kingdom, there is an underlying ethic of building for others instead of ourselves. Inheritance is more than having all of Jesus' stuff for ourselves; it is about constantly adding to the family fund.

FREE MARKET CHURCH

Although free markets exist in capitalist economies, the goal of capitalism is private ownership of means of production and their operation for profit. Free market economic systems, on the other hand, focus on goods, services, and wealth being exchanged between participants through supply and demand.[10] In a brave city, we are not interested in wealth creation and financial sustainability just to pad our pockets or make us independent from others. We are interested in creating resources and sustaining our kingdom life and work. We are dependent upon one another in the deepest and most communal way, but we also acknowledge we must provide something people are looking for. Right now, the church in its present form has lost meaning for millions. The *demand* simply isn't there, and so, the church in its present form will struggle. But new forms of church, the ones that call people beyond materialism, consumerism, and individualism, will slowly gain traction because they intuitively offer a preferable alternative for life, mission, and a calling to the King and his kingdom.

We invite you to consider what's involved in a brave city's free market church ecosystem.

Free: Though it cost him everything on the cross, God gave us Jesus for free. Jesus then gave us the Holy Spirit for free. The Spirit is the source in our lives who directs us on mission (Hebrews 5:9). It's the Spirit who guides us into all truth (John 16:13) and comforts us along the way (John 14:16). That's like getting a personal counselor, a wealth-management advisor, and a wise coach—all for free! The Spirit also gives gifts to all believing men and women (1 Corinthians 12:5–11). The same power that raised Jesus from the dead was given to every believer, and one of the ways it manifests is through unique giftedness to lead, start, grow, and build things that matter. In Matthew 16:19, we learn that Jesus gives us the keys to the kingdom of God. That means that he gives us rhythms of living and the power to bind things that need to be bound and loose things that need to be freed up. That's a lot of real stuff, and it doesn't cost a dime.

Let that sink in.

Oh, there's more. As the church began its most expansive season, God gave the believers simple ecclesial structures he called homes or spaces—simple places where people could meet, pray, listen, worship, and talk about their mission. Although our homes cost money, we don't need to raise additional funds to use them as a space—we are using what we already have. And if we can't afford a sheltered space, we can always meet in the open air, in back rooms of restaurants, in airports, or in coffee shops. In other words, the church can gather without additional costs for a space or structure.

Why did Jesus give us all this stuff for free? To help us avoid succumbing to the consumer-driven priorities of the masses. He also made it all free so that the work of our hands would be less likely to be bought and sold to the highest bidder and corrupted. In real terms, Jesus never wanted you to have to worry about butts on seats or hitting the denominational metrics to keep your job or keep the funding flowing. He never intended for you to sell your soul or bow to a fraudulent form of leadership. He made it all free so that his gift on the cross to set men and women free would make sense. He also made it free so that anyone could join and serve and lead in any part of the world, under any empire, under any duress, and it would always move forward. FREE, FREE, FREE! Church doesn't cost a dime. Like manna in the desert, God provides everything we need. We want you to hear that now, if you've never heard it before.

Market: If we've convinced you that the functions and ministries of the church come without a cost, then what do we do with money? Yes, money is still important, but if all the sacramental functions of the church are free, we can now creatively use kingdom resources and consolidated funds to establish works of blessing and commerce so that "when the righteous prosper, the city rejoices" (Proverbs 11:10). Or, as we saw in the very onset of the church, the collection's main purpose can be so that no one has any need. If free market economics is based upon supply and demand, then we have an open invitation to create something meaningful that people are desperate to find.

Church: Though we don't use the term often, we see "church" as simply the group of people connected to and caring for the city they live in as they share, invest, and leverage all their combined assets to experience and extend the shalom of God to anyone they can.[11] The church was, is, and always will be, the people of God, doing the works of God, for the glory of God.

Remember where we started. This whole thing is art, and

although getting paid for art is great, you don't have to be paid. You can still get a ton of enjoyment and benefit from simply doing it and letting others benefit.

A FINAL WORD ON FUNDRAISING

If you've ever tried to create a new artistic work that needed seed funding, you've for sure run into a situation where it feels like the funders are the kings, and the workers (you) are the peasants or paupers. Often, funding is given with the giver's expectations as a string attached; and the giver's desire to be part of something that qualifies as a "worldly success" becomes a yoke or noose around the artist's neck.

In act one we mentioned Lorenzo de' Medici, who was the Jeff Bezos or the Bill Gates of the fifteenth century. He was wealthy beyond wealthy and could have controlled people with his money. Instead, he was one of history's great "patrons."

Patrons were those who funded artists to do what they did that no one else could. Medici began covering the living expenses of artists like Botticelli and Michelangelo—artists who created works we now consider a quintessential part of the Renaissance.

Most church-planting funds never create new expressions of church because the money is given to people who will reproduce the metrics stipulated by the funders. But patrons don't ask for their interests to be considered at all. They assess the character of the artist and simply trust that they will faithfully use the money for their creative efforts. Now wouldn't it be nice if kingdom funding released apostolic creators to create? Wouldn't it be refreshing if people gave their money (which is God's anyhow) for investment rather than maintenance? That is what it looks like when the manna economy of Jesus supports new works of the kingdom.

Act Five

ORDERS OF DESIRE

Churching Up the Mission—Family Style

More and more, the desire grows in me simply to walk around, greet people, enter their homes, sit on their doorsteps, play ball, and be known as someone who wants to live with them. It is a privilege to have the time to practice the simple ministry of presence. Still, it is not as simple as it seems.

HENRI NOUWEN

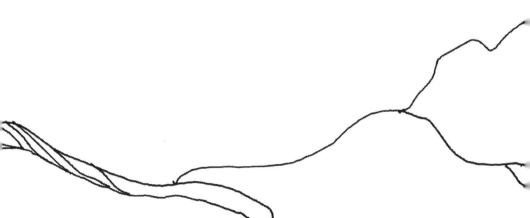

Well, it's finally time to address where most people start. As we've shared this alternative way of being and doing church—in addition to wondering if we "count" having coffee in a coffee shop as "doing church" (which we've talked about in previous acts)—we often get asked some typical questions such as "So, how do you guys gather? How often? Where? Do you all even go to church? What about the historical church and the role of preaching and teaching? What about church discipline? Do you guys ever worship? Do you ever read the Bible?" and a host of other related inquiries.

Before we answer any of those questions, we want to say that we believe disciples of Jesus have always gathered in local communities and identified themselves as "part of the family."

Consider a great family. They do life together, struggle and grow together, share all their stuff, serve people together, and have an intentional dinner together, say, every Thursday. This Thursday night dinner becomes a tradition; it's where everyone can reflect on the week and share their ups and downs. Mom and Dad dispense encouragement and offer timely words of praise. The kids tell funny stories and divulge things happening in their lives. Family members share some Scripture and remember Jesus in an informal communion sort of way. The food is good, the moments are sacred, and in an honest and vulnerable way, Jesus is being praised through all of this.

Now, who wouldn't want to be a part of that family?

But think about that same family-dinner scenario, but rather than being an informal and encouraging time, it's a time when Mom and Dad constantly ask everyone to "be better," question what they could do to be more committed or focused, or put pressure on the family members to "bump it up a notch."

And imagine Mom and Dad meeting with each other periodically throughout the week only to talk about how Thursday nights could be more exciting and more attractive, or how their family dinners could become more like those of the cutting-edge families in the neighborhood. And then, two or three times a year, Mom and

Dad go to conferences specifically designed to teach them the five key steps to improving family dinners.

Or even worse, imagine if one parent makes Thursday nights a dogmatic requirement—like, if you don't come, you're not *really* a part of the family anymore.

If these things happened, eventually the Thursday night family dinner would not be what it originally was.

This metaphor helps us to see that we don't build or grow things based on constantly talking about, analyzing, or critiquing them, or by trying to pressure something to grow. In other words, it does no good to try to figure out if the Lantern Network, The GoodHood, or Love City are "churchy" enough. We should only ask, "Are we being, enjoying, and seeing the fruit of being God's family? Do we look forward to our time together, no matter the form? Do we feel an actual palpable love for everyone at the table? Does everyone know that there is no pressure to come down from their room to join the family meal? Are the people in the family proud to carry the family name? Is the family always excited about bringing non-family members to the table because they want people to meet the family? And are the true spirit, essence, and practices of Jesus being manifested in our midst?"

These are better questions and can help us stay focused on what we *can* do. Since we can't build the church or the kingdom, there's no pressure to manipulate or overthink anything about "church." What is left is an invitation to live for the kingdom and keep digging to find its treasure, both for our nuclear families and for the extended spiritual family we do life with.

Remember, in kingdom ideology and practice, we are archaeologists rather than manipulators. We are artists rather than performers. We are architects rather than executives. We dig for the kingdom together, we listen to the authentic "song" God is giving us, and we build tables together that God uses to construct his kingdom. The pressure is off, but we're motivated to get up early as a family and get at it!

WEIRD CONSIDERATIONS WHEN CHURCH ISN'T FAMILY

If you asked a person in the church of Ephesus or Philippi who the children's pastor was, they would probably look cross-eyed at you and say, "Well, any of us who have kids."

If you asked, "Where do y'all meet?" our guess is they wouldn't tell you, for fear you were a mole trying to screw up their underground status.

If you were looking for a good worship or teaching ministry that was sixty minutes or less, it simply wouldn't be available.

If you were wondering who the leaders or elders were, they would simply point to the members of the family who had the most natural spiritual authority because of their wisdom accumulated through experience, suffering, and study, and their proven integrity over the long haul. For sure, the leaders would not be paid or expected to be at an office where someone could go for help. They would have normal jobs while overseeing the family congregation and holding high the culture that Jesus lived and taught.

These scenarios help us get back to viewing church as a family— and when you finally see it this way, almost everything gets simpler and makes more sense.

Our Western, compartmentalized orientation has really done a number on how we perceive life as a disconnected, isolated series of events. We have seen church as a fourth place we attend, separate from our "normal" lives of home (first), work/school (second), and social spaces (third). Envisioning church as a family means we must remove this fourth-place ideology and integrate it into the first three spaces of normal life. If we don't, our children will continue to separate themselves from us and God's mission.

Our (Taylor's) family motto is to "leave everything better than we found it." Whether that's a room, a family, a neighborhood, or a city. And slowly, our kids are beginning to see that Jesus was the one who taught this lifestyle. Recently we went swimming, and our oldest son invited a friend. Lindsey and I watched as our son basically discipled his buddy. Life on life. Making things better. Bringing good news. He's got a knack for this. But he would have no clue what the term "making disciples" means. He's not an expert yet and doesn't have all the Jesus-lingo quite figured out, but he's getting there. And if we told him he needed to get better at "making disciples" and tried to train him in it, I'm certain it would turn into math for him at best, or even worse, a yoke to carry. But he's witnessed his mom and me and many others around him doing this his whole life. Not only that, but he's been directly involved in the work. The dude is an amazing fisher of people, and it just comes naturally to him. It's not a process or a set of principles; it's a lifestyle. And people tell us everywhere he goes that he just makes things better. He loves and laughs and brings hope in courageous but thirteen-year-old ways. That's the kingdom, and that's a story all of our kids want to be a part of. In the same way, as you model and live a liberated life, bringing good news wherever you go, others will join in. Kind of like Forrest Gump when he jogs across the US.[1] You don't have to prove anything or convince anyone; just run, and other runners will join you.

Milt in the Family

His name is actually Milton Jackson, but once he trusts you a bit, you can call him Milt. About ten years ago, he became a part of our (Taylor's) actual family. Now he's a part of our covenant community, the Lantern Network. Back when we lived in Five Points South in Birmingham, Milt was living on the streets near our house. Often, we would throw parties on our block and invite our friends who slept outside a street away. One cold night in February, we invited Milt. Nine years later, he's still with us. When we came to Alton, to be a part of the story here, Milt did what family members do and moved with us.

Milt was never a number, a project, or a funding opportunity. He was never a metric to prove our efficacy as missionaries. He's just

Milt. Our desire was to get to know Milt and others like him; and because we were asking God to lead us, one day we heard God say, "Invite Milt in." So we did. Milt has some significant needs, so others help us care for him at times. If we're out of town or busy with other things, our brave-city community tries to handle getting Milt his five insulin shots a day and cares for the other normal things that go along with someone his age who's had more than his share of hard times.

Like Birmingham and most other cities, Alton has had to figure out what to do with our homeless population. We've told you about the warming center one of our community members started, and we've been able to employ many homeless persons in different businesses in our network—but civic, political, and church groups still grapple with how to fix the systemic issues such as mental health or drug addiction that often perpetuate the problem. Hundreds of millions of dollars are spent every year by non-profits, churches, and government agencies trying to effect solutions. Still, in cities across the nation, it appears that homelessness is not only getting worse but is also headed in a direction that may not be reversible. So, what's a better approach?

You spread out the need among families. As we framed out our kingdom ecosystem—this new "city within our city"—it became a network of tables and families where people not only get help, but they also, and more importantly, become part of us. As Paul taught in Ephesians 1:5–6, we aren't converted to a religion as much as we are adopted into a family.

Milt may go down in the Lantern Network's history as one of our best evangelists—because he's initiated more parties than anyone else in the community. He loves to barbecue. Nothing special, but the man knows meat. When Milt cooks, you get dry-rub ribs, chicken, beef, and sides of mac and cheese that will put you in the hospital. Every time there's anything to celebrate, Milt calls for a party. And it happens. People may say no to other recreational offers, but when Milt calls it, you go. The neighbors show up, and the kids show up, and Milt puts on a spread.

We share the story of Milt because if you can see how naturally a homeless man can integrate into a family, then you have found your answer to almost every dilemma of how to grow a church or handle the challenges in your city. The church needs to be an extended family to the world. We don't believe in "outreach"— that's just doing something short term and only serves as a Band-Aid. We believe everything Jesus taught was meant to equip us to be his family. If, at the end of the day, you're not willing to let the person you're presently trying to help become a part of your family, or for you to become a part of theirs, then the result will often be negligible.

An Order, Not a Club

With the "family" as our overarching image of what church is, consider another aspect of how the family lives its life together. As we fleshed out in act four, we think of a brave city as a sort of new monastic order. We're not talking about a cloistered community that isolates itself like a country club—with membership requirements, gatherings for meetings, and a collective identity based on their name, style, doctrine, social preferences, and a clear sense of who's in and out.

Instead, think of a group of people whose aim is to bless the population by the work of their hands. One such group is the modern-day "order" connected to a brave city in Aliquippa, Pennsylvania, where people have been living together and financially supporting and sustaining an affordable housing community. These men and women have literally committed their lives to this town and are deeply respected there. They are handing down both their assets and their way of life as they live out their faith.

The leader of this community taught Taylor and me about monastic life, sharing with us that, "An order is a 'community of desire.'" In other words, they join their lives together because they want the same things. For example, they may desire to do "works" together—like many historical monks, or they may desire to be with the poor.

Thinking about the church as a familial "community of desire" is important because it will completely reframe the tone, cadence, and even metrics of success. If your desires are for the poor, it's not that you just want to work *for* the poor; it's that you desire to be *with* the poor. And that makes a world of difference in how a community lives out its works in the world. For instance, some of our friends received a $20,000 grant to put toward transitional housing for the homeless. At first, they set out to find one home they could all use for folks who were coming through their different businesses and works. But as they talked, they realized that many of their leaders desired to not just work for the homeless or help them in short fits and starts, but that instead, they desired to be *with* them. So, rather than forming one house that could be used for a homeless program, they helped make significant renovations to four people's homes so that there would be four families taking in new family members.

Other kingdom ecosystems may desire to "renew ruined cities," as Isaiah 61 proclaims. This shared desire will probably lead them to see success in the actual restoration of spaces for their town.

Thinking of church as a familial order helps with our confusion about how churches should grow. Do we add more "churchy" stuff—gatherings, and programs—and invite people to events? Or do we ask people to just come join the order? To pray with us, serve with us, renovate homes with us, and start businesses with us. Most monastic orders feel no pressure to grow unless someone shows up wanting to join them in their life of loving and serving others. Thus, the normal pressures or metrics of growth don't even cross their minds. They are simply there to help people process their desires and help them move more deeply into those desires.

A person can only fight against the currents of worldly life for so long alone. So spiritual growth must be about finding a community that helps us resist those currents and keeps us moving forward. We believe, as Jesus did, that individualized spirituality isn't strong enough to help us accomplish this. We don't believe that Jesus allows us to discover him by ourselves. So, finding a family that shares your desires is a far better option, as it will encourage movement in the right direction, and the spiritual formation will be far more transformative.

Let's talk now about how "family intentions" can help us to be a familial "community of desire."

FAMILY INTENTIONS AND DESIRES

When you begin to think of church as a city within a city, or an interconnected and interdependent ecosystem of familial enterprises, businesses, justice works, missional communities, or simply "good works," you'll find that things just grow. However, familial growth is very different from organizational growth. Let that statement sink in for a second. People want to join the family and get around all the family tables you have created. Because of this, you won't need to over-organize but you will need to have some *intentions*—just like a mother or father does for their family. If you're a parent, you know you can't force growth in your children, but there are hundreds of intentional moves you can make that help foster that growth. And so, in the same way, we should talk about some intentions you can have as your ecosystem grows.

A healthy family sets doable rhythms, atmosphere, expectations, and cadence for developing the family members, for handling adversity as well as sin and human frailty, and for helping people to create a worldview and personal identity. As the nuclear family becomes less and less the norm—whether through divorce, fostering, or incarceration—welcoming people into an extended family gives us the best shot at recovering a biblical, kingdom-oriented community.

Consider how the family handles the following.

Crisis Management

When someone is sick, or they find themselves with a blown water main, or they hear some strange noises going on in the house, they might call the church office, an expensive plumber, or the police. In our brave city, our ecosystem, we call the brothers, sisters, moms, and dads. Reda has emerged as the HVAC specialist. Dr. Deedee is our on-call physician for over-the-phone diagnoses. Matthew, Hugh's son-in-law and Alton firefighter, responds when kids crack their heads open on the trampoline. Jesse, Hugh's other son-in-law, gets the call when the McCall kids hear something strange in the basement and Mom and Dad are out for dinner. Taylor gets tapped for anything tool-related or when something needs hauling with a truck. Tammy gets the call when we can't figure out what to do with unique homeless or poverty situations. As any vibrant and inter-connected community should, we have Bible teachers, shepherds, counselors, musicians, cooks, and party throwers. And on and on. We occasionally have to "outsource" some specific need that is above our pay grade, but in almost every situation of crisis, we've got it handled inside the family.

In Matthew 6:25–34, Jesus talks about worry and encourages us not to even bother with it. We assume he was speaking in the context of a community of people who are following him together. Notice what he says at the end: "But seek first his kingdom and his righteousness, and all these things will be given to you as well" (v. 33). The kingdom is the remedy. In Mark 10:17–31, Jesus said that if we give up the things of this world for the sake of the kingdom, we will be given a hundredfold in return. We don't think Jesus meant we'd get one hundred cars (or any other kind of riches). We think he meant that, in this kingdom economy, if Taylor's car breaks down, he has access to Hugh's car, or David's car, and so on.

Crisis by nature is something that evokes worry and panic. To just say "trust God" to a friend whose daughter can't breathe well, or a young woman whose ex-boyfriend has just threatened to find her and kill her, or when a father loses his job and can't seem to find a new one, is just too simplistic. Jesus, in framing everything under the idea of seeking first his kingdom, was assuming you were seeking as a community. So, "Don't worry because the Rileys have a car and can get your daughter to the hospital within five minutes"; or, "Don't worry, Sara. Hugh and Taylor will be right over to sit with you and stay the night if we need to, so you'll feel safe from your ex-boyfriend"; or, "Bill, don't worry, man, if you can't find a job this month—we've got you covered and can help you with rent and other bills." This is why, in a kingdom city, people really do worry less.

Evangelism

Evangelism really is simply "heralding good news"—so, somewhere along the way, we just started believing that we could do that all day, every day, as a spiritual family.

Hugh, a natural evangelist, walks around the coffee shop in his spare time, looking for people who have become "regulars" over the past few months. He walks up, smiles, and says, "Hey, it looks like you're getting to be a part of the family here. I see you've been coming in for months, but I haven't been able to get to know you. Would you mind giving me two minutes of your story?" These two-minute stories usually end up being about thirty minutes, and most people ask Hugh for a bit of his story, giving him the opportunity to talk about his family's move to Alton and why they opened Post Commons. He seems to be able to talk about the kingdom in ways that just make sense to people. He's also been asked to be an "adjunct" spiritual father at his CrossFit gym.

Hugh has been connecting with folks for many years, so some think he's unusually gifted with that ability. But what does this look like for the rest of us? Consider our manager at Post Commons, who struck up a conversation with Hank, a young single dad who just came in for coffee. Over the years, they had a few hundred more conversations. When I (Taylor) saw Hank recently, he was sitting out at one of our tables reading the Bible. He stopped me to tell me he had found faith in God. Consider Jesse, who coaches football at our high school and had one of his players ask him about how to find God. Consider Lindsey and me, who wouldn't say we are gifted evangelists, but we have seen quite a few people come to faith as they live with us. Consider a young woman named Chris, who came to faith by watching the Halters struggle in losing their son. Consider Rachelle, who found the kingdom story through Natalie and Justine, who hired her as a barista. Consider the fifteen young boys who now play on our "beyond basketball" team, who have now heard the story of God from the coaches who share not only the message of Jesus but also their entire lives with these fatherless youth. Consider Sterling, Joe, and Chris, day-laborers who are hearing about the kingdom as they work on a residential redevelopment. Or consider the young men and women who come into Rodney's makerspace and end up being apprenticed in telling their story through craft. They also hear of God every time they eat Sunday lunch with Rodney and his wife, Julie. Evangelism has become as natural as waking up and going to work, and it aligns with the early church expectation that people will come to us to ask us about the hope we have (1 Peter 3:15).

Teaching

"When do you teach? How do you teach?" We get the teaching question all the time. Recently, Hugh and I were working with some leaders in Philly, and a guy brought it up again. So I asked him if he had a family. He said yes. "What ages are your kids?" I continued. "Seven, nine, and fourteen." So I said, "Do they know about Jesus? Are they familiar with or even regularly exposed to the Scriptures? And are they being discipled?" He answered yes, to all of these. Then I asked him what day of the week he did those things. He was silent for a moment, and then the penny dropped. I told him that I realized long ago that the good news and the truth of the Scriptures are inside of me, and my five kiddos don't need to hear weekly lectures on how they can apply that to their lives. They just need to see it and have it taught to them in the natural flow of our everyday life. Still, that requires some focused intentionality and regular interaction. So why can't that be applied to our spiritual families as well? Could the problem be that we're just trying to get as many people in a room as possible or to prop ourselves up as the ultimate authority who tells others how to think? Something seems backward and anti-family about this picture.

Although present church forms elevate and separate the teaching ministry from the average Joe and Jolene, we think the work of teaching is one of the easiest to decentralize to everyone. It would be pretty weird to ask your nuclear family to meet once a week for thirty minutes to hear you preach a sermon (like the fictional family example we started this act with). So we don't try to do that with our spiritual family either. Instead, we share thoughts from Scripture in an email loop to the community; Cheryl (Hugh's wife) links in our family and a few friends in a daily devotion teaching; we facilitate a men's twice-monthly journeymen gathering at Post Commons; and on Sundays, usually a few of our homes are open for coffee and a simple question of "Does anyone have a word from God for us today?" Then we share Scripture, talk about it, share what's going on in our lives, and talk some more. So, our teaching ministry happens all week long.

Discipleship

By now, you can tell that discipleship happens just like raising kids. We teach only what we need to, when it's needed. Any other type of discipleship—through a set curriculum or study guide that is not timely—will be forgotten. This takes the pressure off and leads us not to teach but to guide, just like a mother or father would. You know, of course, that when parents try to teach a concept, it mostly is met with rolling eyes from a child. But when a child is in trouble or runs into something at school that is upsetting or confusing and feels trust and desire to share it with a brother or sister, mother or father, it creates a better opportunity to deal with questions that lead to them taking ownership over a discipleship issue in their life. We all know that the worst form of learning and retaining is simply to sit and hear someone talk about a subject. But somewhere along the way, we turned this into discipleship—whether it's a Sunday morning lecture or a 6 a.m. "discipleship" meeting at Starbucks. It almost feels like we took our cues from the Industrial Revolution and said, "How can we run as many people as possible through our assembly-line discipleship programs to get the most payoff?"

But here's a reality about spiritual formation (discipleship): people only grow when they are in tension. Often, people only change when they get caught and have to face the reality of their sin. Or they just get exhausted from the same fight with their spouse over and over, so out of desperation, they finally call for a counselor. Or they have tried to medicate the pain away through booze or weed or even worse and have come to their "end." This is where real discipleship happens. In sword making, metal is heated to a "nonmagnetic" temperature, so that it is pliable, and it hardens the material, creating better wear resistance and significantly more resilience.[2] Think about that. We too are being forged and refined by fire, and the crucible is everyday life. Together, as we fight the pull and power of the world, we become less drawn to its ways, more pliable, and develop the resilience and endurance needed for a kingdom life.

Discipleship is simply learning to believe and live out the ways of Jesus. The goal isn't just to convince someone to believe in Jesus; the goal is to get them to believe what Jesus believes. And if they truly believe all that Jesus believes, their behavior will change naturally. This is why life-on-life in real life is Jesus' model for true discipleship. A class or two doesn't hurt, but it isn't enough.

Church Discipline

This one has always been a head-scratcher for us. We're not sure if you know this, but the Reformation had a profound impact, now and then, on the perceived role of the church. The reformers reframed the church around three primary duties: the right preaching of the Word (as determined, of course, by those doing the preaching), the right administration of the sacraments (administered, that is, only by the male ordained leader), and the correct execution of church discipline.[3] So imagine you've been stuck in the legalism and corruption of the Catholic church system, and then Martin Luther and the boys say, "Hey we've got a better way to do this church thing," and so you, like any curious observer, respond by saying, "Oh, great. I always thought the Catholic way was a bit weird, so I'd love to hear your ideas." And then the reformers say, "The church is where you go to hear us teach, give you Communion, and where we spank you when you screw up."

What would you think? That may seem like an overly simplistic, tongue-in-cheek rendering, but we've studied church history, and we have to say, we believe it's pretty spot on.

But out of these three pillars of the reformed church—which, by the way, were taken on by many non-reformed traditions as well—perhaps the one that is the hardest to understand is the church discipline part.

In our day, I think we can all acknowledge that people in the church have learned never to share deep, dark secrets because, in the end, they will be outed or asked to leave. We do not have a good process for healing and helping those wrestling with sexual perversion and pornography, marital affairs and discord, substance abuse, anger and rage in the home, or any other human struggle. As the church gets more organized, more institutionalized, and more public, it seems we only get better at covering up the mistakes of our leaders and parishioners—or shaming them for messing up in the first place. It's built into the system.

Our past and present forms of "discipline" have therefore fallen short and may not represent the true spirit of how to help people come clean and get the help they need.

Now consider church as a family. If you have a family member—say, a son or daughter—choosing to live a life contrary to the ways of Jesus, do you guilt or shame them? Do you make them do some penance based on the severity of the infraction? Do you kick the child out of the home? Not if you can help it! What you learn in a family are the nuances of timing, how to get a hearing, how best to challenge and encourage, when to hit hard and when to back off, when to allow them to experience natural consequences, when to completely let them off the hook, how to point them to Jesus, and how to model grace so that they always know they can come to you with any issue. That's a great family.

When kids are young, they need some rules and some appropriate punishment; but as they grow, parents learn that no matter how bad the infraction or sin, children must be given the opportunity to take ownership and feel the weight of their own decisions. So you turn in your rod, staff, and law tablets, and instead become the mom and dad sitting on the porch looking to the end of the driveway for a struggling prodigal to return.

But what about what Jesus says about conflict resolution and church discipline in Matthew 18? Well, here's what Lindsey and I (Taylor) have always taught our kids (and, in turn, others): You're gonna get pissed at folks. They're going to say something to offend you and rub you the wrong way. *Do not* trash them behind their backs; that's just petty and never really helps anything. *Do not* go to them right away. It's just plain annoying. Take some time to cool off. Around 70 percent of the time, you'll realize the person meant nothing by it; you're just too sensitive or having a bad day, and you read into it, and you should get over it. About 28 percent of the time, you'll realize what happened or what was said was a little out-of-pocket or careless, but you know them, and you know their heart and the totality of their life, so you get over it. The last 2 percent of the time you just can't seem to let it go; you lie awake at night thinking about it, and resentment builds up. So you have to work up the courage to go to them and find out if what you heard and are thinking is correct, and then work through it together. Sometimes that doesn't work, so you need to bring a trusted friend or two into the conversation. If the problem is really bad, you might need the help of the whole family. But the goal is always restoration.

But what about 1 Corinthians 5:1–5, where Paul tells us to expel immoral family members? This is a tough one because it's virtually impossible for us to imagine kicking one of our kids (or family members) out of the family. But I have seen it come to that, and if it does, it should be one of the hardest and most painful moments of your life. For instance, in extreme cases of physical abuse or threatened abuse, there have been times we've had to tell someone they're not welcome. But the thought of wanting a family or spiritual family member to experience shame, pain, or a feeling of abandonment seems totally unlike Jesus and the kingdom. So, God forbid, if this ever does happen to your community or movement, it should feel almost like a funeral. And the day even a ray of repentance, a desire for reconciliation, or a posture of humility comes over that person, should be like the day the prodigal finally comes home. It's grounds for a party (see Luke 5:11–32). The father didn't need to know if the son was sincere; he just wanted him back in the family.

Societal and Political Conflicts

Speaking of failures, there may be no bigger miss in the organized church than how to navigate all the tensions between our faith and the world's customs.

Paul begged the Ephesians to fight for unity (Ephesians 4:3), and Jesus said that the world would see the real deal in the love his disciples had for one another (John 13:35). But the atmosphere inside the kingdom city isn't like the 2021 riot at the US Capitol, where people were fighting for control so that their values could be secured. In a brave city, people find what they can't find anywhere else on earth: God's peace between people. Whereas many US denominations have split over the LGBTQ+ issue, the woke issue, the Black Lives Matter issue, or the Republican vs Democrat issue, inside a brave city, we see all these different types of people bringing their differing opinions and beliefs to the King and letting him rule. In a brave city, we want to be family-oriented, kingdom-focused, and Jesus-centered. We don't need everyone to believe all the same things in order to hold ourselves together. The leaders of most present-day brave cities don't tell people what to believe and don't expect agreement on everything. They just put good works, kingdom works, justice works, and Jesus at the center, and let other issues take care of themselves.

If we become bound to dogma, we forget how to love our neighbors, and we lose sight of the importance of kingdom works with Jesus at the center. We forget how to include people in our midst who think differently from us because we are so focused on trying to get them to believe the right things. In brave cities, a missionary named Jesus teaches us how to focus on the main things (love and good deeds) and trust him for all the gray areas as we follow him. Jesus knew that to lead with judgment doesn't produce the fruit that kindness does, for "God's kindness is intended to lead you to repentance" (Romans 2:4). He also knew that you never get a change of behavior unless you first get a change of heart and soul, and that only happens through friendship. And so, as he did with the woman who was caught in adultery (John 8:1–11), we don't let people's sins cause us to separate from them. Instead, as Jesus did, we advocate for the sinner. And when in doubt, we go with the perfect law of love as the new hinge point of the kingdom of God (Matthew 22:37–40). As Jesus said, all the law and the prophets now hang on these two commandments: to love God with all that we have and to love our neighbors as much as we love ourselves—without asking for them to believe or behave as we do.

If the scriptural mandate is to love our neighbors as much as we love ourselves, that means if we discover a neighbor is gay, smokes a lot of weed, screams at their children, or throws benders every Saturday night till 2 a.m., it doesn't affect our desire and ability to love them. Healthy families don't make broad-brush statements of affirmation or condemnation of lifestyles. If someone asks us what our stance is on a subject, then we only have to speak for ourselves, not our entire congregation or political party. We may not agree, but we also don't have to condemn. We don't have to live like others live, but we also don't have to impose our moral imperatives on them. Church as a family means we expect *not* to agree, even inside our church community, about all these issues, so we share our opinions, but we don't have to become opinionated. We might be politically concerned and active on certain issues, but we don't have to become political.

Political parties, denominations, and institutionally focused churches have very little positive pull in changing the world, but a network of families does. Although it's not a quick and easy answer, the church as a family does have legitimate answers—from the homeless problem to the sin problem. The only thing that is needed is a real family.

THE HAMMER, THE TABLE, AND THE GRANDMOTHER (DISCIPLESHIP'S BIG THREE)

A couple of years back, I (Taylor) was a part of a missionary think tank with other practitioners around the country. One of our exercises was to discuss building a disciple-making culture and the tools that are needed to do that. I reflected on the more than twenty years I have been involved in kingdom excavating, living in three different cities, and working in countries all over the world. And the tools I landed on were the hammer, the table, and the grandmother.

The *hammer* is the Monday through Saturday life. It's the building, the digging, the creativity, and the innovation. Work is better together with your family, and families grow better when they work together. Just a few days ago, I spent ten straight hours on a Sunday working with my sons. First, we cut up a tree, split it into firewood, and stacked it along our fence. The stack was sixty feet long and four feet high. So, you can imagine how much wood that was. Then we spent the rest of the day cutting grass. Recently the boys started a lawn business, so I've been working with them and teaching them the tricks of the trade. I love working with them because I know there's no better environment for them to see who I really am—how I work, how I respond to adversity, and how I treat them (my "subordinates"). While we are together, I look for teachable moments, moments of levity and laughter, and moments to express gratitude for the work we get to do. But what I learn from them might be even more valuable: their goofiness, the way they turn everything into a game, their pure competitive spirit, and their brotherhood. It reinforces the idea that discipleship is a mutual trade-off. No one is *the discipler*. We're all mutual disciples of Jesus, and we learn from him and one another. Sure, I'm further along in my journey, and they look up to me, but I'm learning from them more than they know. In the end, if we try to be or make disciples without the context of actual work, I fear we will keep missing the mark.

The *table*, as we've already talked about, refers to both the spaces we build as well as the rest and remembrance we cultivate in those spaces. If the hammer is the building of the convergent spaces, the table is the intentional use of those spaces, where we as a family rest, learn, eat, drink, and play. When Rodney used his literal hammer to build Soulcraft—the woodworking mentorship shop—he didn't stop there. As we said when discussing evangelism, he extended the hammer into a table by inviting his mentees to his house for weekly table time where he could let go, let down, ask more pointed questions, give more specific encouragement, and help these young men and women cultivate a vision for life, work, rest, and a healthy rhythm of relating to God.

The term *grandmother* refers to the elders among us—the calm in the storm and the steady hand of the body. Only recently have I begun to understand the importance and necessity of the grandparent or the elder. In 2016, I found myself in Standing Rock, North Dakota, during the pipeline crisis among the Lakota people. A group of us knew what was happening and simply felt led to make our way there and listen to their struggle. I could share many things about this trip, but one of the more indelible marks it left on me was the presence of the grandmothers: their countenance and stability, their courage and patience, their ability to laugh at the surrounding troubles while holding the deep, painful memories with grace. Though I was able to have conversations with some, I still needed to understand more. Since then, I have pored over material about indigenous cultures and traditions: their family structures, their concepts of honor and virtue, and their undeniable reliance on their grandmothers. It wasn't the powerful leader and commander role that was needed from them; it was their stillness, their presence, and their keen understanding of the principalities and powers at work. They had been through it all—success, failure, happiness, despair, betrayal, and lifelong loyalty—and had come out on the other side. They knew things weren't ever as bad as they seemed. And when the sky was falling, they would just smile and hold everything together.

As I've traveled all over and worked with zealous apostolic movements trying to build something real and authentically "of the kingdom," I've concluded that the lack of spiritual grandparents (*presbuteros* in Greek) is one of the most significant gaps in our missional circles. I don't blame any singular group for this. I wouldn't say it's the elders' fault or the young passionate leaders' fault. It just is. And it must be addressed.

So, the hammer is where disciples are made by working together as a family. It's where our lives are reproduced, and how we show what we really value. The table is where we come together as a family to rest, remember, and solidify the truths that were revealed in the work. And the grandparents are the ones who quietly hold the family together through their presence, their consistency, and their wisdom.

INVITING INTO FAMILY INSTEAD OF CHURCH SERVICES

Let's go back to where most people begin when it comes to churching up something. We have shared some ideas about how a decentralized movement can gather, but now think about what would happen if people weren't invited to attend a church service but were instead invited to join intentional familial "orders of desire," who use their hammers to work together, who create tables to celebrate and rest together, and who are led by the wisdom of the family grandmothers.

The founder or initiating apostolic leader could easily call everyone together, even weekly. For the sake of argument, let's say Hugh tells everyone, "Hey, let's add a weekly gathering at the Post Commons building." Everyone would probably be interested enough to come and might even invite friends—but the large gathering, set by the apostolic leader, may just end up being a reflection of that one person.

Instead, think about a scenario where six to eight decentralized kingdom families working together throughout the week all have weekly or biweekly "family dinners" together. If those families also carry the responsibility of inviting the larger community to their tables four times a year (or whatever seemed to fit), these families would be discipled into regular rhythms of working and creating spaces of rest and celebration together, but they would also interact with the larger community. As a result, many more people would be invited to family tables, and the larger community would be blessed by experiencing many other qualities of these unique families. We believe those diverse connections would not only grow the leaders of the kingdom ecosystem, but they would also set in motion a truly decentralized, but connected, family—ecclesial style.

"

A PERSON CAN ONLY FIGHT AGAINST THE CURRENTS
OF WORLDLY LIFE FOR SO LONG ALONE. SO
SPIRITUAL GROWTH MUST BE ABOUT FINDING
A COMMUNITY THAT HELPS US RESIST THOSE
CURRENTS AND KEEPS US MOVING FORWARD.

"

Act Six

KINGDOM ECCLESIOLOGY

All the "Churchy" Stuff You've Been Wondering About

Every human wish and dream that is injected into the Christian community is a hindrance to genuine community and must be banished if genuine community is to survive. He who loves his dream of community more than the Christian community itself becomes a destroyer of the latter, even though his personal intentions may be ever so honest and earnest and sacrificial.
DIETRICH BONHOEFFER

In June 2022, Roe v. Wade, the legislation that made access to an abortion a federal right in the US, was overturned. If you peeked your head out and gave your opinion—or even crazier, tried to lead your congregation to all take the same stance—you might remember that it didn't go well. There used to be a day in the typical evangelical church when we had so few differences that we spent our time making up things to separate over—like eschatology, second baptism, charismatic gifts, or whether Amy Grant was a real Christian. Yes, we did argue about the interpretation of certain Bible verses, but essentially everyone could find a tribe that believed roughly the same things. You could put your Anglican, Presbyterian, or Baptist signs out and attract folks who already agreed with most of your preaching. But now, with cancel culture in society and the church, one of my (Hugh's) pastor friends exclaimed, "Those days are over!" He filled in his story like this:

> Five years ago, I was living my dream. Our church was a successful church plant at seven years old. We were the new cool church, and even though we put a lot of effort into Sunday gatherings, we theologically bought into the missional movement. We were trying to transition small groups into more engaged missional communities, had a pretty multiethnic staff that represented our city better than most churches, and had some great local and international justice works our church was involved with. Quite frankly, I thought God's favor was on us. And even if it wasn't, I was having fun! I enjoyed the weekly rhythm of sermon prep, and our staff was so solid I barely had to get involved in all the other day-to-day church stuff. Now, after Trump, COVID-19, race issues, gay issues, and now the abortion issue, our church is down to its last 20 percent. Oh, and by the way, we're Southern Baptists, so we lose another 5 to 10 percent after each national scandal and sex scandal surfaces in our denomination. And I've come to realize I have no real authority; people really don't care what I think, or what they think I think the Bible says about an

issue. They only want to hear what they already believe. I'm not sure how much longer I'll be hanging on. It just seems like a silly charade.

Maybe some or all of this resonates with what you've experienced. And maybe, like this leader, you've been wondering how to remain faithful in whatever leadership role you still have. But the bigger issue now is what real influence, true authority, and practical leadership look like in a brave city.

You probably know by now that leadership and influence no longer flow from one's position on the organizational charts or the fact that one's Sunday services are well-attended. You're probably also aware that numerous denominations have been struggling to respond to current cultural issues with biblical faithfulness. But when a top-down organization tries to speak, decide, or hand down broad-brush positions that their leaders or congregants must adhere to, it no longer holds any weight. Even worse is when a church expects their beliefs to be accepted by broader society. Though many churches believe they are doing the right thing in speaking up against society's ills, we think it goes against the grain of what Jesus was calling us to do when he gave us the Great Commission. Jesus had influence on both those inside and outside the faith, and he gave us that same authority when he said in Matthew 28:18–19, "All authority in heaven and on earth has been given to me. Therefore go and make disciples of all nations." However, the Great Commission doesn't mean we are to impose our Christian beliefs, forms, or moral code on others or coerce them to attend our weekend services by using the fear of hell.

Jesus' words in Matthew 28:18–19 represent a key moment for Jesus in passing on his kingdom initiative, and they are based solely on the concept of authority. Jesus knew then, and most of us know now, that doing anything for Jesus without that authority will always fall short (see John 15:5). Jesus wants us to have the authority and ability to influence people, so he gave that authority to us intentionally. Luke 4:32 says people who heard Jesus were amazed at his teaching "because his words had authority," so we are to seek to be leaders who operate with that same spiritual authority. But it's important to remember that his type of authority doesn't come from a title, position, salary, or denominational sanction.

Even though Jesus had authority, multitudes also abandoned him when they didn't like what he had to say. So don't view authority in terms of how many people follow you or how well you think your sermon went this week. There are three things on which authority can be based: fear, position, or evidence. Jesus said that his work provided evidence of his authority: "Do not believe me unless I do the works of my Father. But if I do them, even though you do not believe me, believe the works, that you may know and understand that the Father is in me, and I in the Father" (John 10:37–38). Jesus desires to see similar evidence-based authority in us, but it takes time to grow.

Thus, in brave cities, we try to move away from anything that smacks of fleshly effort, coercion, branding, fearmongering, or selling something. Instead, we internalize the gospel, in our hearts "revere Christ as Lord" (1 Peter 3:13), and commit to do good works and be a faithful community. As we do so, we hope that, in due time, people take notice and give us authority to go into new places and woo people toward our way of life and the Author of this new life. As people show an interest in Jesus, we teach them more and help them to make Christ Lord over every part of their lives. In a brave city or kingdom community, there is no need for coercion, groupthink, or statements on where we all stand on every issue— because each of us learn and take ownership of both our faith and the Lord's timing of how it plays out in our lives.

So when it comes to establishing true authority among both believers and seekers, we need to explore four key thoughts about natural spiritual influence. Some of these affect the stability of our faith community, some affect who and how we should lead, some affect gatherings, and some affect what we measure as real success.

INFLUENCE THROUGH STABILITY

There are many things you can easily do to fill a room full with people. There are also quick and easy ways to empty the room. Multitudes come and go like the wind. Our hope in brave cities is less about how many are in the room and more about how we are growing and holding together a committed group of people based on a common struggle and mission. With this end in mind, stability is far more important than charisma. Stability is the ability to hold course, regardless of the winds and waves of change. Stability is not living in a safe harbor with no waves, anchored to a dock that is held in place by forty-foot piers. Stability is the internal ability of the vessel to handle the tempests when it has pulled up its anchor and finds itself in the open water.

Many churches view their moorings as church tradition and the Bible, but in reality, disunity can quickly come, simply because of different interpretations of specific Bible verses. So although God's Word must be a part of what forms our stability, we cannot simply say, "The Bible holds us together." We bring this up because we want you to focus on the internal stability, faithfulness, and spiritual integrity of the vessels (the people) instead of thinking your church mission statement, the Nicene Creed, or denominational historical statements will unify you.

Even a strong vision doesn't bring stability. As we've charted out new brave cities, the initial team often struggles to understand what is being built. When there's no specific church service at the end of the week and there are no programs to plug kids into, people start asking for us as pioneers to tell them exactly where we're going, what the vision is, how long it will take, and if there will be any costs. All of these are great questions but, if you've ever gotten a vision from God for a city, you'll realize that you have pictures in your mind of what God could do, and it can be incredibly hard to clearly share those visions and pictures with others.

So, in brave cities, where do we find our stability?

Our stability is found in Jesus' faithfulness to us. Sure, that might sound simplistic, but every brave city leader we know talks about God drawing them to or exposing them to the needs of a specific town or part of a town. Then they talk about unique relational and financial connections that happened that they could not have pulled off on their own. It becomes very clear, as you watch and listen to how brave cities are formed, that Jesus was the initiator and supplier of 95 percent of what happened. So we have to stop recruiting people to our vision and instead tell the story of how it happened. If you can get those looking to join you to believe in Jesus and his leading, they'll be more apt to hang in when the road map gets a little fuzzy.

When one young man told Jesus he wanted to follow him, Jesus responded with a rather puzzling comment. He said, "The son of man has no place to lay his head" (Matthew 8:20). This was more than an attempt to confuse or frustrate this would-be disciple. I mean, surely the guy knew that Jesus' mom's house was right down the street. What Jesus was doing was framing what life is like on mission with him. It's not about just one night without a hotel. Jesus was trying to help this young man understand a bigger issue: that we may never feel as though we've got a place to lay our heads. People want to know where they'll lay their heads, where the best schools are for their kids, what the best investments are for a good return on their money, and where all the new housing developments are going in, so they'll know where to plant a new church. But brave cities go where other people don't want to go. We go to the cities that have descended, not the ones that are ascending. We go where a localized church with tithing members probably won't happen or happen anytime soon. We are a people who keep fighting for the good things of the kingdom, even if we're not seeing any traditional measurements of success. But notice that Jesus, while challenging this young man, also knew that he would provide spiritual stability for him. To Jesus, risk and stability can exist at the same time.

When starting new church expressions, there's got to be an honest conversation about the future and making five- to ten-year plans. We're wondering if that kind of long-range planning may actually be a sin. Yes, there are Bible verses that encourage foresight and making plans, but always within a Middle-Eastern construct of "as the Lord wills." If the COVID-19 pandemic taught us anything, it is that we must be filled with hope, but not think that we know the future enough to say, "Today or tomorrow we'll go to this or that city, spend a year there, carry on business and make money"; Scripture instructs us that it's better to say, "If it is the Lord's will, we live and do this or that" (James 4:13–15).

Once you see this, you start to realize how strategic Jesus' teaching on prayer was: "Give us today our daily bread" (Matthew 6:11). This *manna provision,* which we explained in act four, is also a *manna mission principle.* As we go where God sends us, we must look for and disciple people he brings into our paths without knowing all the details or what the outcome will be. We just remain faithful to God's mission for a city. There are people who will commit to God's mission even though we never get them "plugged in," and people who find stability with Jesus and his community as their anchor instead of a system of church programs.

Too many leaders who have attributed their plans to a vision from God find themselves backpedaling for a number of reasons. It's very convenient to use, "God told me …" as a means of attracting or drawing followers to a vision, but it's also dangerous to suggest that God is leading what we want to lead; or that he is leading us into something that is going to be a wild success; or, if the vision ends prematurely, that we missed the boat and somehow didn't fulfill the mission God gave us. I (Hugh) remember, after the end of our fourteen-year Denver church plant, people said, "Oh, see, Halter's thing didn't even work." And I remember thinking, "Damn! We had a fantastic fourteen-year run! That was the most fun, most fruitful, and best decade and a half of my life!" To the onlookers, there was no way we experienced success, but to me, there was no way it was a failure. As we try to interpret God's intention for his church, it doesn't seem like longevity is a key goal or plumb line of success. The early church was formed as apostles moved from place to place, planting seeds of the gospel and trusting God would make those seeds grow. Our work is therefore about obediently architecting the good works of the future kingdom. Are we having an impact? Are we preparing and sending missionaries? Have we tilled up the hard soil for the next ones God will send here? Are we setting foundations that others can build on? Have we been faithful in responding to God's leading to date? These seem like the right questions.

Rather than formulating grandiose plans that focus on success and longevity, it is far more faithful to simply say, "It seems good to us and hopefully the Holy Spirit that we should do this today and trust him for tomorrow" (see Acts 15:28). What we're trying to say is that the desire for stability is more about faithfulness to God and less about safety and worldly wins. His way is the way of risk. The safest place we can be is in the den of lions, as long as he's in there with us. In a brave city, we accept what God gives us with open hands. Whether we are in the same place for fifty years or a new place every year, we are stable because our foundation is on Christ.

Our stability is found in spiritual family. We need the spiritual moms, dads, big brothers, and big sisters who know how to sail rough seas and who give encouragement, courage, and faith to the younger disciples as they put their hand to the wheel. Spiritual stability comes from spiritual moms and dads who help us remain faithful to God, even when we can't see what's ahead. Moms and dads hold the family together, nurture, train up, bear with, and empower the family. This is why the leaders are called *overseers* in Scripture. (See Acts 20:28, Philippians 1:1, and 1 Timothy 3:1.) Overseers don't plug people into church programs or try to pander to their wants and desires for security. Overseers, or the elder community, are the ones on the front line, looking the fearful, tired, cold, and traumatized soldiers in the eyes and holding them together. Why do they bring stability to the community? Because they are still on the front lines and have been in a handful of battles already. They know the lessons, they know the signs, they understand the strategy, and they've been in the fight long enough to encourage the rest to keep going. They may not know all the details but they know enough to steady the hands and hearts of the community.

You can see that these elders are different from the run-of-the-mill elder you might find in a local church. True eldership is based on the natural authority someone's earned by following the Holy Spirit into mission. Plain and simple, these will be the most important people in a brave city, not because they have any title, salary, or position. It is because they have none of these but still hold weight and have the gravitas to move people to a new future.

Just know this: There is no foolproof way to keep bad things from happening; no iron-clad guarantee that you'll have smooth sailing or perfect stability when you are doing kingdom work. Everything rises and falls on the depth, maturity, and gifts of your community far more than on the institutional frameworks. People are everything.

INFLUENCE THROUGH SERVANT LEADERSHIP

Right now, most people don't trust those in positions of power, and if you want to recognize and assert this type of authority, you'll almost always lose—and lose big.

Lance Ford, in his book *Unleader*, shares that, "Depending on the translation, at the very most, 'leader' is used only six times in the New Testament, while the word 'servant' can be found over two hundred times."[1] That alone should help us sniff out why the typical American church is going through so much trouble. Actually, most pastors we know are humble, simple-hearted, and love the Lord. We don't see in most churches the misogynistic, celebrity-minded, power-hungry leaders we see in the media. We think they are few and far between, but we do see that the solo leader, senior pastor, executive pastor, and the like are still digging holes in which land mines can be placed. We don't need to waste time talking about all the issues, but if you are trying to be a leader and move volunteer adults into a cohesive, totally unified movement, you know it's like selling ice to Eskimos.

As pastors, people may like us and may even brag to their friends about their "pastor," but when push comes to shove, they'll leave you if you preach a challenging sermon, have a bad day, or—heaven forbid—verbalize your human struggles with women, men, doubt, porn, addiction, materialism, or other similar issues. People may say they want good leaders, but they will stop following the moment the leader neglects to give them what they want. Real leadership comes from servants who live a life so undeniably authentic that some people simply can't help but follow.

This is why act seven of this book focuses on the lives of apostolically gifted people. They end up as the leaders, but the only ones who keep going for the long haul are those who serve the movement and recognize they can't own it, control it, or secure its eternal lifespan. In a real sense, they have to work harder and give more, but they do it without a dog in the hunt other than their hopes for people and for the kingdom to be manifest.

The Clergy-Laity Dilemma

We've preached and taught about the clergy-laity division ad nauseam, yet there are still those who believe the clergy should do almost everything while everyone else is equipped to do very little. The only way that the laity will be priests is if the priests become laity. Said another way, if you eliminate the clergy class, then you've simultaneously eliminated the laity class. And when you've finally gotten rid of both classes or categories, what's left are people who serve Jesus, regardless of whether they are paid or not—the real servant leaders.

The word "laity" comes from the Greek word *laos*, which means "people." So let's keep it that way. Just people. This is why we suggest you never take any money for ministry. Take money for coaching, training, entrepreneurial ventures, bettering the city, or time spent working with your hands in some way. But don't take money for teaching, singing, discipling, pastoring, crisis management, hospital calls, or the normal jobs of the "pastor." God's people can do all this!

Membership

There is no evidence of church membership in Scripture or any historical movements of the church until the last hundred years. Membership seems to be an attempt to get more buy-in or give more perks, but this "country club" organizational structure tends toward arrogance, control, or guilt, and not toward growing disciples. Servant leaders don't lead by controlling people through "membership." If your more intentional way of life isn't a draw to them, trust us, they will leave with or without membership. And if your way of life is compelling, they will keep moving deeper into the story and in their faith, so you have no need to create a designation for a certain "level" of commitment.

If trends continue, and the church looks and lives more like a brave city, you'll see even more people move toward the monastic-order orientation we've advocated—where covenants and rules of life form a pathway of intentionality instead of old membership arrangements.

Giftings, Functions, and APEST Servanthood

If the clergy and laity become unified and everyone is highly committed, then we no longer need titles or positions. What remains are God-given giftings. People will therefore operate and be known in the community for their unique contribution born of God's thumbprint on their lives.

Ephesians 4 tells us that when all the members (*laos*) are properly working together, the body grows up into maturity, to the stature of the fullness of Christ. When we look at the early church (and every other Jesus-movement that has had a notable impact throughout history), we see that everyone is regarded as a significant agent of the King and is encouraged to find their place in the unfolding of the movement. In other words, in the church that Jesus built, everyone gets to play. In fact, everyone must play—whether they be an apostle, prophet, evangelist, shepherd, or teacher. But before reading the verses below, consider a rarely discussed aspect of this text. The vast majority of the time, this passage is read as a *leadership* text. In other words, we have normally understood the gifts that are mentioned to be given to those who lead the church for the purpose of equipping the rest of the people of God. However, one of the most revolutionary aspects of Ephesians 4 is that it is not a leadership text—it is a text about the *ministry* of the church. It is a *body of Christ* text. Paul is stating that the gifts given to the church are actually given to the *laos*—the whole people of God.

> As a prisoner for the Lord, then, I urge you to live a life worthy of the calling you have received. Be completely humble and gentle; be patient, bearing with one another in love. Make every effort to keep the unity of the Spirit through the bond of peace. There is one body and one Spirit, just as you were called to one hope when you were called; one Lord, one faith, one baptism; one God and Father of all, who is over all and through all and in all.
>
> But to each one of us grace has been given as Christ apportioned it. This is why it says:
>
> > "When he ascended on high,
> > he took many captives
> > and gave gifts to his people."
>
> (What Does "he ascended" mean except that he also descended to the lower, earthly regions? He who descended is the very one who ascended higher than all the heavens, in order to fill the whole

universe.) So, Christ himself gave the apostles, the prophets, the evangelists, the pastors and teachers, to equip his people for works of service, so that the body of Christ may be built up until we all reach unity in the faith and in the knowledge of the Son of God and become mature, attaining to the whole measure of the fullness of Christ.

Then we will no longer be infants, tossed back and forth by the waves, and blown here and there by every wind of teaching and by the cunning and craftiness of people in their deceitful scheming. Instead, speaking the truth in love, we will grow to become in every respect the mature body of him who is the head, that is, Christ. From him the whole body, joined and held together by every supporting ligament, grows and builds itself up in love, as each part does its work

EPHESIANS 4:1-16

Positions/Titles

If we take Ephesians 4 seriously, we are probably wise to do away with titles altogether. Just use your first names, and let people describe to others what you do inside the community. "Hugh sort of started this whole thing and is the dad around here. Lindsey kind of 'holds everything together.' Sam gets dreams for the community, and McKenna lights up every room she enters and usually has a friend in tow." We don't lead with titles or positions of power but by serving one another with our giftings.

Many folks agree with and operate using the present-day model of eldership, but after working with thousands of churches and over sixty denominations, we can tell you without reservation that the most debilitating and paralyzing aspect of "high forms" of church, even in the lowlands of Mississippi, are the elders. Not that these people, most often men, aren't good people who love God, but they usually defend past traditions, worry about political fallout, protect their own positions, and work to preserve the present forms. There are understandable aspects to this, but when you are trying to build out a truly entrepreneurial network based upon the apostolic and prophetic nudges of God, these are not the things you want people thinking or worrying about. The other elephant in the eldership room is simply the fact that they are not modeling a way of life you are calling others to. Thus the movement stops. As we suggested, a few stouthearted grandmothers can out-lead most megachurch elders in true community, authority, and wisdom from the trenches.

INFLUENCE THROUGH GATHERINGS

We've spent the first part of "churching it up" focusing on people, because so many have acted and believed that the main thing that holds God's people together is a church gathering. Now that you know we don't think this is the case, let's take a new look at the why and why nots, and the when and when nots, of gathering people together. Gathering God's people together has historically always been the most dangerous part of church life. Someone once said, "Christians are a lot like mice: If you see just one all by itself, it can be sort of cute, but if you fill up an entire room with them, it will freak the hell out of you!" Why? The more people in one spot, the greater the potential for trouble. Different opinions, styles, expectations, hopes, and dreams all converge to create an impossible stew of disunity. If you ever want to have fun, google, "Crazy things that happen in church." I (Hugh) won't tell you all the things you'll find there, but my favorite was a worship team that added a "creative" element: an older man on skates doing those dance numbers we all remember from back in the 80s at the local roller-rink.

In just my own church gathering history, I've watched a man drop his pants and pee in the middle aisle while I was preaching. Another man stood right in front of me with the double bird flipping me off for thirty minutes. (I must not have trained my elders very well.) I've seen a woman leading worship who was so beautiful that men asked me later never to have her on stage again. I've seen interpretive dancers, flag ensembles, snake handlers, crazy preachers, and prophetic singers who start yelling at people. I've seen a woman go under water in baptism in a white sheet with absolutely no underclothing. I've endured hundreds of terrible sermons (many of which were my own) and even worse "special music numbers." I've consumed way too many of those ubiquitous communion wafers with the thimble-sized plastic cups that the kids then use to make cracking plastic noises for the rest of the service. Oh, and then there are the parents who think it's cute when their toddlers come down and tear their diapers off at the front of the church while you're trying to make your final point. I guess I could go on, and I'm sure you could add a few of your own favorite anecdotes.

But, for crying out loud, most of us still think that getting a large group of relative strangers together to sing and listen to a lecture is the pinnacle experience of the Jesus people. What's more, many of us judge a person's commitment to God almost entirely on whether they attend the Sunday morning, Sunday evening, and Wednesday evening services. Good grief! It's as if knowing and following Jesus has become completely identified with church gathering. Years ago, Lindsey and I (Taylor) noticed that any time you tried to talk to someone about Jesus, they would immediately turn the conversation to the location they drove to weekly to attend one of these gatherings. It was as if Jesus, his mission, and his unbelievable good news were no longer on anyone's minds. Instead, the point seemed to be what organization and theological construct they were a part of. Sort of like they had thrown out the baby and kept the bath water.

I'm not sure if you've ever heard of the Celtic Christians, who were highly influential between the fifth and eighth centuries. They were the folks who re-Christianized the world after the institutional church of Rome was sacked. Almost one century after Constantine instituted the places of worship and appointed priests to guide the community into rote practices (which formed sanctioned worship), the Celtic Christians instead centered the worship of the church around the "cell" (or inner-life communal practices) and the "coracle," which was the actual medium for mission.[2] The coracle was a small, rounded boat. Missionaries (normal people) would get into that boat and shove off toward unchartered territory. They had no place of worship, no priests to guide them, and no formal ceremonies. No Hillsong, Bethel, or Hosanna music to entertain them. Wherever their coracle touched the shore, they set up businesses, farms, and houses, and contextualized their core communal practices into the pagan landscape they found themselves in.[3] Did they sing? Sure, but was a weekend time of listening to a lecture and singing three songs a central part of their activities? No. Not even close. Their lives were communal in work, devotion, service, and spiritual practices that made sense to their unique contexts and calling.[4]

Like those ancient missionaries, it's time for us to recalibrate worship as a communal work of presenting our bodies as living sacrifices, as we "coracle" our way around a city or town together, and we learn the "cell" spiritual practices that make sense for our own missional community.

Some brave city ecosystems buy homes that serve as twenty-four-seven places of prayer and worship. Some have a monthly time of gathering that may have several hundred folks, alongside weekly times in homes with just ten folks. Some have no formal gatherings except house gatherings. And some, like our own, are a combination of leadership gatherings during the week, optional worship-only gatherings every month or two, home gatherings, spiritual retreats, and additional gatherings for Christmas, Easter, St. Paddy's Day, children's birthdays, weddings, baptisms, work parties (like the old barn raisings), and straight-up bashes just to have fun together.

As you can see, if someone were to accuse us of "forsaking the assembling of ourselves together," as Hebrews 10:25 KJV says, we'd be able to refute that notion with a pretty robust gathering schedule. Some will insist that this verse is about worship gatherings, and all our other stuff doesn't count; but that verse doesn't mention worship gatherings. In fact, the context of Hebrews 10 is that, because of Christ's new and living way (as opposed to the Old Testament system of priestly sacrifices), we can draw near to God, spur each other on toward love and good deeds, and gather in any way we are able. Remember, in the Old Testament, God wanted the people to give a portion of their increase to fund parties and festivals (see Deuteronomy 14:22–26). We love the spirit of what God seems to be after. People need jubilee and gatherings where their loads become lighter, and they can see glimpses of God's future world.

The Speakeasy Church

Five years into our story in Alton, we had our first gathering of seekers. Prior to that, we had leadership gatherings for our workers, and private meetings with owners who started businesses, justice works, or neighborhood communities. We also had dinners, parties, and private conversations with many seekers. But for five years, we never called them all together—until Christmas Eve of 2021. Prior to that, we weren't sure if we had the street cred, the respect, or had earned the right to invite anyone anywhere. Instead, we were a spiritual speakeasy.

Speakeasys, of course, were unmarked homes and businesses that served as underground gathering spots for people to enjoy booze and carry on their normal social functions during the prohibition years.[5] Attendees often had to perform a secret hand gesture or speak some predetermined phrase to enter. People trusted friends to invite other friends and keep out those who were bent on exposing their illegal network. Of course, we are not hosting illegal Jesus-gatherings, but there are some important similarities. We, like many brave city ecosystems, feel that the Jesus part of our mission needs to be held closer to our chests. Often, church planters are trained to go into towns and actively recruit Christians to their new brand of church. We've seen this happen for decades now and have been guilty of it as well. But we are challenging apostolic missionaries to take a different posture. We want to lead with good works and good people and wait for those in the community to show interest in the spiritual part of what we do.

We have also been completely uninterested in growth for its own sake, and believe Jesus knew what he was talking about when he said, "Be on your guard against the yeast of the Pharisees" (Matthew 16:6). We think it's time for small, highly focused Christian movements to take their cues from monastic orders and start making it difficult for people to become consumers of religious goods and services without taking on the life of God's people. This protects the movement of the brave city, and it is the best way to serve and disciple those who are looking for something different than just a church to attend.

In Alton, our strategy was to start with good business, build a great team, bless as many people as we could, and work for the peace of the city. Over a five-year span—through our public offerings and private invitations to dinners, parties, and activities—unique tables of connection happened. Over time, people started to ask us about our faith, shared their own faith or lack of faith, and made it crystal clear they wanted to be at our table. When enough of this movement was happening, it made sense to call a big party for Christmas Eve. The invites went out, and the recipients said they were honored to get them.

As we gathered, we simply welcomed our guests, shared how we all had become friends, and made a point of saying that there was no organization or church behind the event. Then we invited everyone to reflect on the story of God coming to earth. It was beautiful, simple, and profound; and we didn't invite them back to anything the next week. What we know, however, is that people trust and respect us, and many of them are close friends whom we love, and they love us. As stewards, we created visions where workers could help create tables, and where seekers could find hope and life with us. When you live every day in an interconnected ecosystem, where the people you want to be exposed to the hope of Jesus and the kingdom are coming to your tables every day, you're not dependent on a weekly manufactured church experience.

It may sound weird, but if you survey the most prolific Christian movements, you'll find they were spiritual speakeasies. The underground church of China and the Middle East, the Celtic Christians, and the early church in the first three centuries all carried on without a brand, without a church name, without a place to gather consumers, and without an "official" person to lead them. Their only brand identity was that they were God's people. It's crazy to think that our denominational brand identities took a thousand years to even show up on the scene. Perhaps in the future, we may finally move away from those brand identities and instead see the emergence of relational communities based on their missional identity.

The early church grew as people were drawn to people, the quality of the community, and the works of this countercultural band of Jesus-followers. This is not weird; it's just not the lens through which so many have been looking at the church. Consider the potential if you have no public brand or church name, no one answers to any certain leader who is everyone's pastor, and you don't have to center church life around a building. What you're left with are natural conversations and drawing people to Jesus and his way of life. This configuration has no insiders or outsiders, no churched or unchurched, no religious or secular. There are just friends becoming closer by doing good works and learning about the Author of all that is good.

As these kingdom ecosystems are beginning to develop, they often function as nonprofit or business networks from which the speakeasy-Jesus-community forms. There are no names for these communities and gatherings of Jesus-followers. This protects us from being overwhelmed by consumer Christianity—the "leaven of the Pharisee"—that can come in and screw up a good loaf of bread.

Bottom line: You'll either attract seekers and repel consumer Christians, or you'll repel seekers and attract consumer Christians. You need to design a community that repels who you don't want in order to attract who you do want. You don't need a name or a brand for this; you just need good people who are doing good works and who speak the name and story of Jesus.

Sacraments of Life

Organizational church has taken sacraments and made them special acts that can only be performed by ordained ministers in specific gatherings. But sacraments that reveal God's grace can be done anywhere by anyone.

Sacraments have been some of the most powerful and misused elements of Christian life throughout the centuries. The *Merriam-Webster Dictionary* defines a sacrament as "a Christian rite (such as baptism or the Eucharist) that is believed to have been ordained by Christ and that is held to be a means of divine grace or to be a sign or symbol of a spiritual reality."[6] Did you catch that simple, powerful meaning? It is a Christian "rite" or repeatable act "ordained" or sanctioned by Jesus; and, as we participate in these sacraments, the world sees the reality of God's grace. In the past it might have been baptism, the Eucharist, praying for the sick, or penance; but in our day, here are some sacraments we think most accurately align with this definition:

- **Availability:** Restructuring life so you have time for the life of Jesus in his timing. This often means pursuing downward mobility to free up time that can be an actual training and discipleship metric.
- **Neighboring:** Taking care of those in close proximity to us—or taking them into our family. This is caring for the "closest places."

- **Generosity, Hospitality, and Sharing:** Loving the stranger and offering anything we have to anyone who needs what we have.
- **Sharing the Lord's Supper:** Remembering Jesus whenever we intentionally eat and drink together. Celebrating Communion always happens around a good meal or a good toast.
- **Living with the poor (those with limited access):** Prioritizing who Jesus prioritized and remembering the least in every decision we make. This will affect where we choose to live.
- **Sabbathing in Community:** Resting and remembering Jesus together. If there's anything that seems to bring all of Jesus' repeatable sacraments into alignment, it's communal rest and remembering Jesus.

David, who runs Post Commons, also started Idle Roasting Co. and used a sabbath experience to name and brand the roaster. Here's his description of Idle Roasting from their website:

> To be honest, we struggled to find a name that conveyed what we were trying to build. When we finally got our roaster installed, we put the first batch through and decided to meet the next morning to try it. We all had busy, full days ahead, but we carved out time to connect over the first roast of coffee. It was then we realized that moments like those make coffee special. Moments in your car on the way to work, moments with close friends at your favorite spot, or the moments sipping on a cup in the comfort of your home with family and friends. These moments force you to slow down, collect ourselves, listen, and reflect.[7]

Even though we may not have weekly "church services" to administer "special sacraments" in Alton, we do gather consistently, with our children, to dive deeper into everyday sacraments that reflect God's grace. It's a growing, morphing rhythm—and some times are shorter, some times are longer—but regardless, it's natural.

A Few More Considerations About Gatherings

Gatherings of any and all kinds should only exist to the extent that the entire network feels they are necessary to hold people together or to propel the community forward. Gatherings can be for training, relational connection, and learning, as well as for rest. Therefore, some gatherings ought to be an opportunity to take a break from the mission field, recharge, and get ready to go back to the field. We also find that it is wise not to lock yourself into something forever. Stay flexible about how often and how long you gather and take breaks when they are needed.

Obviously, centralized buildings are not the problem. In fact, in building kingdom ecosystems, space-making is a central strategy. But the difference is that the spaces we make are not set apart or considered sacred because we worship there; they are sacred because God calls us to create missions with buildings and spaces. Our coffee shop is sacred, our farm is sacred, our barbershop is sacred. "The earth is the LORD's, and everything in it, the world, and all who live in it" (Psalm 24:1).

To boil this down, we think gatherings should be about the mission, not the individual. Time together supports missionaries, not consumers. And, just in case you wondered, missionaries don't need as much singing as you might expect. They need coaching, encouragement, witness from other missionaries, and empowerment. And yes, musical worship can be important if it is thought through contextually for your movement; but firing up the band because you think the church needs it is a misstep. Music is important to mission—in mourning, in celebration, in preparation for battle, or even just in helping individuals build performance skills. It's an incredible tool that I (Taylor) find myself in awe of.

But as a recovering worship leader, trust me, good music without mission draws consumers that will slow the movement, whereas focusing on broader elements of missionary edification and development will allow you to figure out the most creative ways to hold your people together.

INFLUENCE THROUGH METRICS

As you can tell, we have a high view of the activity of the church, not as embodied by a Sunday-centric focused ministry, but rather as reflected in the life of Jesus and in how we see the early communities prioritizing the mission of God. Our sacramental practices reflect this, as does our desire to see the church behave more like a family than an institution. So how do we know if anything is working? How do we know if we're on the right track? These are normal and good questions. The answer is, we keep track of things—we measure things. It'd be weird if we didn't care about hitting some target.

Whatever you measure is what is meaningful to you; and whatever is most meaningful will be what you manage and work toward. So, if you measure success by butts on seats, online views, sermon downloads, or budgets, you'll focus on growing those areas and potentially achieve success according to those metrics. For example, if the room is full of people, they might give enough to help you fund putting your sermons online. And the folks who like your online sermons might actually pay for subscriptions that will help you hire more staff who can run more classes and provide more services for people. And then you might be able to multiply into other campuses where rooms keep filling up … and so on and so on.

But, if you remember the bear story from act two, you'll recall that we were making the point that we must find and follow Jesus in the wild. Jesus rarely seemed to measure what we measure, and he often looked for things we rarely look for. One way or the other, we will measure something, so we want to figure out what Jesus cares about—what he would measure.

Beyond that, even if we are hitting our stated metrics, we are often not producing the type of person the world is glad to have as its neighbors. So, often the problem isn't metrics; it's *what* we are measuring.

Consider a few paraphrased scriptures to help us get at what matters:

- "Do not say, 'Today or tomorrow we'll go here to this town and do this or that.' ... Instead say, 'If it is the Lord's will, we will do this or that'" (James 4:13, 15). What does this say about future planning and trying to attract people with lofty visions? How do we keep a balance of faithful, hopeful prayers and dreams to see things move and grow yet not get too far out in front of God?
- "If you are trying to please people, you cannot be a servant of Christ" (Galatians 1:10). What does this say about our attempts to pander to donors or consumer-church shoppers? How might this affect the pressure we feel to cast a perfect vision before those who may fund or participate in what we do?
- "You cannot serve both God and money" (Matthew 6:24). What does this say about how we make decisions about money and our call to risk and trust? Where is the line, especially in business, between saving and securing operating cash versus sacrificial giving—the kind of giving that hurts—to meet the needs of those we see around us?
- "The way of the kingdom is narrow" (Matthew 7:14). What does this say about reproducing ankle-deep spiritual experiences for people or chasing growth and large gatherings instead of seeking deep personal transformation? What aspects of our vision and community life will most people not want to sign up for, but are what we feel we must stay true to?
- "What is Paul? And what is Apollos? We just did what God said. I planted, he watered, but God did the real work. He

just let us help out" (1 Corinthians 3:5–9). What challenge does this passage offer in regard to our focus on titles, roles, job descriptions, and our posture of leadership in the communities we serve? This passage may truly be the best plumb line for our faithful work because it tells us we have no ability to grow anything. And yet to this day, there are people who are considered "church growth experts." These verses also indicate that we never quite know where our work sits within the totality of God's work in an individual's life. So sometimes we lead off, sometimes we find ourselves at the end of the order, and sometimes we bat clean up. The key is that the work God has assigned us is what we will and should be focused on. Did we work with God? If we did, then we must be content with our part in whatever results occur.

To continue to base our ministry on old-school metrics, such as attendance and baptisms, seems to miss almost all the things Jesus would focus on. In 1 Corinthians 1:13–17, Paul is lamenting how people use baptisms to fight over who is the greatest leader. He seems to be downplaying his own baptism numbers and, in the end, gets to the point, "For Christ did not send me to baptize, but to preach the gospel" (v. 17).

All serious communities have "intentions," so we hope taking time to challenge false and unhelpful metrics not only takes some pressure off all of those who lead but also keeps the focus on working toward more natural, organic growth.

One way to think of this is to concentrate more on the "soil" or the ways we prepare the soil for the seed. What are we doing to soften hearts, lay the groundwork, or give nutrients to help nurture kingdom ways and architect kingdom structures in our city?

We should also remember that most natural growth, if it's healthy, is slow. In the Western church, we love fast growth. *Outreach* magazine always has an annual issue on the "fastest growing churches," and when you read the details, the clear message is that the right things grow the fastest ... or at the very least, we should be impressed with the leaders of congregations that grow quickly.[8]

The reality is that healthy human spiritual growth rarely happens quickly. Helping one couple through a hard marriage, supporting a young man through alcoholism, or wooing an atheist neighbor to be open to talking about spiritual things all take a lot of reps. And if growth happens too quickly, it's often unhealthy for leaders as well. A not-so-secret side effect of rapid growth is how exhausted the leaders of these fast-growing churches often are. They are frequently so tired that they have no energy for their neighbors—or even their own families. Even within the microchurch movement, you'll find exhausted leaders trying to multiply communities. The problem isn't the size; the problem is the preoccupation with growth.

Here's another truism: You always reproduce who you are. So, if you're a church-service person, you'll probably eventually invite a few more folks to a church service. But if you're a "righteous one," and you care most about bringing justice and mercy to those who need it, you'll probably attract a few more folks to that way of life. One is quick and one is slow, but you can see how much more bang for the buck there is in doing small, hard things slowly versus doing big, easy things fast. One builds *our* kingdoms, and the other bears witness to *his* kingdom.

When thinking about metrics, also think of personal character. Jesus didn't promise that following him would be without trouble, physical toll, or even death. So, in human terms, if you follow Jesus, you will have some rough days. But the way of Jesus should also be lived without anxiety (Philippians 4:6), even when facing slander or persecution. Jesus taught us not to even fear death. Our hard work and tough times can and should be faced without anxiousness or loss of sleep.

Remember that there are certain things only the Spirit has the ability to do, such as convict people of sin, righteousness, and judgment (John 16:8–11); only God can cause growth

(1 Corinthians 3:5–7). That should alleviate any pressure we might feel about whether or not someone decides to believe in Jesus or clean up their lives. Add in the fact that we cannot grow anything in the Spirit at all … that takes a lot of weight off, doesn't it? Imagine if you could live a life not worrying the tiniest bit about anything (see Matthew 6:24–34)—especially whether the thing you're doing grows or how people respond. Boom! Now we have the freedom to just live according to the ways of the kingdom, being blown away at all the things God does because of our faithfulness and intentionality.

What should our success metrics be? What should we be focusing on and measuring? All the things this act has been talking about. Allowing God to do a deeper work. Being available all day long to people and needs that come our way. Looking to change the atmosphere of a home, a street, or a town through the good works and good people you do life with. Hearing the joyful sound of laughter coming off the front porch of one of the homes in your ecosystem. Knowing the coffee shop you opened provided someone a free place to work and meet people. Finding yourself in a community that communicates daily, responds to needs that come up, and shares all things so that no one has any real need.

How do we know if we're on the right path? Jesus said you'll know them by their fruit (Matthew 7:20), and you'll know them by the love they have for one another (John 13:35). If you have those two things, you can be pretty sure you're over the target zone.

Act Seven

APOSTOLICING

The Life of a Pioneer Servant

Consequently, you are no longer foreigners and strangers,
but fellow citizens with God's people and also members of
his household built upon the foundations of the apostles and
prophets, with Christ Jesus himself as the chief cornerstone.
EPHESIANS 2:19–20

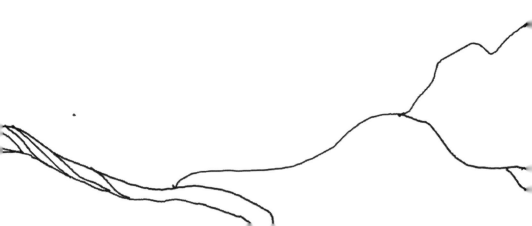

Taylor and I have often discussed how hard it is to help people understand our role, or function, in the brave cities we've led. Often people will come into Post Commons and walk up to me and say, "Are you the owner?" My response is usually, "Oh no ... I was just the one who started all this." And if I have more time, I usually talk about the first year when I spent most of my time "behind the curtain," working with my hands to renovate the building that has become our apostolic center.

Right now, we need to talk about you—the pioneer or pioneering community that starts everything. Whether male or female, old or young, experienced or greenhorn, there is a certain type of person who is uniquely gifted and called to start things from scratch. Luke 14:28–29 is a great lead-in passage for this discussion: "Suppose one of you wants to build a tower. Won't you first sit down and estimate the cost to see if you have enough money to complete it? For if you lay a foundation and are not able to finish it, everyone who sees it will ridicule you." In our context, "counting the cost" is fundamentally about following Jesus. Building a tower is one thing, but consider how much more applicable this is for those of us who get spiritual inklings in our hearts to attempt a significant start-up work for Jesus.

This entire book is about apostolic works and apostolic movements, which require apostolic leaders. The word "apostolic" generally describes ones who are sent out by someone,[1] but our focus here is on the *first ones* sent—the pioneer force that begins *ex nihilo* (out of nothing), and then stirs up kingdom dust that God builds upon. It's no wonder that, in Ephesians 2:20, Paul mentions that God's household, his city, is "built on the foundation of the apostles and prophets."

In our day, many have come to think that the shepherds and teachers should run the church, and that the church is only a shepherding and teaching game. There's nothing more incorrect and culpable in causing the church to be anemic and immature. While shepherds and teachers are essential for the church, they cannot be so to the exclusion of the evangelists, prophets, and apostles. All the giftings fulfill critical roles; but, for whatever reason, 1 Corinthians 12:28 says "God has placed in the church first of all apostles, second prophets and third teachers." This ordering isn't about which gift is *better*; it's about *strategy*, and the simple fact is, to start new things, you must begin with pioneering leadership. This "new wine and new wineskin" formation (Matthew 9:17) will always be specifically put upon those who get the vision first, start working first, suffer first, and lay the foundations for all that will be built later.

A dear friend of ours, Neil Cole, once gave us a great picture of the apostolic being like a thumb. Though a hand obviously needs all the fingers working together, the thumb is unique because it can touch all the other fingers and works with them to get things done. There are many good books now on the APEST orientation, so if you want to learn how all the other gifts (fingers) operate, we suggest the work of Alan Hirsch and Neil Cole.[2] But to see the church as a city within a city, or a kingdom ecosystem that is constantly growing and bearing fruit, we must focus on the thumb—those with the apostolic gifting and lifestyle, and how the brave city forms around these gifts and functions.

The apostolic gifting and function can be seen primarily in those pioneers who "steward" the "builders" and "seekers." Practically, the apostolic ones are the people who wake up in the middle of the night with a dream they can't get rid of. They are the ones who often need to shrug off the well-meaning advice of their friends who try to discourage them from pursuing their new visions. These focused leaders tend to be catalytic. They envision possibilities and identify a work that needs to be accomplished. As primary entrepreneurs, they must establish the essential links between funding, vision, team growth, and community engagement. They have a discerning sense of what would be considered an aroma of Christ versus the stench of religion. The apostolic ones are the cultural architects who model the new way, create attainable forms that inspire others, and unify everything essential to establish and propel the mission forward.

Recently, my (Taylor's) wife was with our youngest son at a school event. A teacher asked him, "What does your daddy do?" He said, "Um, I think he builds a lot of things and gives them away." His response made us laugh because none of my kids really know what to call what I do. But his description was profound because he said what I would want to inspire any pioneer servant to give their life to. There are many ways to look at the apostolic, but it shouldn't be viewed as a position or as a title. Instead, it should be viewed as an essence of Jesus, as a gift, as a personality, and as a work. As an apostle himself, Paul calls himself a wise builder and a foundation layer (1 Corinthians 3:10).

Because apostles tend to be the initiators of a vast relational and spiritual network, they therefore hold a dangerous role in people's lives. People put huge trust in them as the ones they follow, and often the apostles become *ad hoc* spiritual fathers and mothers. But because they never stop building, people can feel abandoned and hurt when they move on to something new. This is where shepherds are needed to come alongside those carrying out the vision to provide nurture and care. And that's why the pioneering work can be so messy and hard … and why the cost should be counted.

Remember, the first one through the wall always gets bloody! So if we call the apostolically oriented ones anything, let's call them "frontline overseers." They are the ones who count the cost, who see the risk, but usually don't have the money or the ability to pull off the vision. They are forgotten in success but blamed for failure; they take the heat and the shots, but after considering everything, they still move forward by faith and get to work.

MODERN DAY *SHALIAH*: THE NEW APOSTOLIC FORM AND FUNCTION

Recently we discovered some unique Jewish history that used a very specific term for apostolic leaders: *shaliah*—which literally means "emissary" or "messenger." This person was also a legal agent. Accordingly, a *shaliah* performed acts of legal significance for the benefit of the client, as opposed to him or herself. *Shaliah* is a Hebrew term comparable to the Greek word *apostolos*, the root of the English word "apostle." A *shaliah* has been described as:

- one who assists in the Jewish rite of circumcision by holding the child upon his knees;
- one who is interested in a child's welfare, and in some measures may take the place of a father;
- one who may be appointed to betroth a woman on another's behalf and who may accept betrothal on behalf of the woman;
- one who may be appointed to deliver a divorce document to a man's wife, and who may receive it on behalf of the woman;
- one who may be appointed to purchase or sell merchandise on another's behalf or to effect an act of legal acquisition or transfer of ownership.[3]

If the *shaliah* is any example, it's clear that the apostolic functions carry great responsibility. Each day is a Spirit-led journey, filled with many different tasks that God builds upon. When Hugh spent ten months renovating the Post Commons building, meeting with city leaders, identifying the initial team, forming relationships, establishing legal and administrative functions, developing the board, creating deep interpersonal connections, and more ... he was simply building a skeleton that would support all the future muscles and functions of the body. If leaders around you question the necessity of modern-day apostolic work, remember that *shaliahs* do not act independently; they are emissaries *sent* to perform functions and complete tasks the Father gives them to do. Below are a few of the named sent ones from the New Testament accounts:

- Barnabas (Acts 14)
- Andronicus (Romans 16:7)

- Junia, a woman (Romans 16:7)
- Epaphroditus (Philippians 2:25)
- Silas (1 Thessalonians 1:1, 2:6)
- Timothy (1 Thessalonians 1:1, 2:6)

So, let's boil it down. The apostle is the one God sends to perform the functions needed to broker a host of important activities that foster a new community. Think of them like a godfather—not in the Al Pacino sense of a mob boss, but in the sense of the grandfather or grandmother in the community or the trusted emissary sent by the king to do the king's work. Apostolically gifted leaders are emissaries sent on behalf of the Father who sent the Son who sent the Holy Spirit, to create living bridges between heaven and earth, emissaries with no guile or personal dog in the hunt. They just go because they love the Father and love the ones the Father still pursues—the lost and hurting.

APOSTOLIC COSTS

Please don't get too excited about this apostolic function or role. It's the most necessary role to start a new community, but it comes with some serious costs. In Luke 14, when Jesus talked about a builder counting the cost, he implied that they must know exactly what they are getting into because being a godfather, an emissary, or the agent who brings everything and everyone together essentially puts them in the crosshairs, both of demonic forces and the worst actions of humanity.

I (Hugh) was traveling in Australia with a man whom everyone referred to as one of the country's apostolic leaders. We were talking about wine, Australian culture, crocodiles, and all sorts of wisdom down under, and I asked, "So what do you think is the true mark of apostolic leaders?" He laughed and blurted out, "Suffering, of course." As we talked more about our lives, I felt a strange encouragement that someone had finally given me a context for why apostles suffer and how important it is in our development, and for our street credibility and spiritual moxie. Of course, there are unique aspects of suffering for those gifted in all the APEST functions; and even for all who answer the basic call to follow Jesus, but as we continue, we want to hone in on the specific things we think you, as a pioneering leader, should know are coming.

The Cost of Religious Critique

The 2022 FTX Super Bowl ad, with comedian and television producer Larry David, is a humorous look at how many great ideas were shot down throughout history.[4] It starts with an ancient entrepreneur demonstrating how a "round wheel" works better than dragging big stones across the ground. Briefly considering the new option, the leader says, "I don't think so … one of the worst ideas I've ever heard." Then another man presents the idea of a fork but gets mocked by someone who points to their ten fingers and says, "I got ten forks fork right here." There's Alexander Hamilton's drafting of the Declaration of Independence and the idea of allowing everyone to have a vote, which leads to one of the farmers questioning the idea by saying, "Even the stupid ones get to vote?" Then you see Edison showing the lightbulb, followed by portable stereos, Walkman music machines, and computers—all similarly rejected. The spot ends with the challenge not to scoff at the idea of cryptocurrency as a new form of exchange. It's sort of ironic that FTX, the company behind the ad, ended up being fraudulent and filing for bankruptcy.

You get the point; new ideas, often for good reason, face scrutiny and resistance. In the same way, stakeholders in traditional forms of church rarely see the benefit of change or the need for nuanced missional expressions. When a denominational leader looks at a brave city's construct, they often ask for "proof of concept" before they want to take the risk of sanctioning or financially backing an out-of-the-box idea. When present forms of church are proven to be failing, it seems unfair that the adventurers have to prove their concepts before they'll be backed, but that's the reality. And even when we can get potential partners to fund or join us, often their participation comes with strings attached. It's a means to control or keep the new vision within the bounds of the old, which never works. Thus, religious critique might sound like, "Why do we need more churches in our area?" It may come in an expectation that you'll offer a particular style of worship, or through making funding conditional on the mission becoming a "real church," or by a roll of the eyes on why you are starting a business instead of a teaching service on Sunday.

The Cost of Spiritual Warfare

Besides the normal unconscious and conscious opposition to new things, apostolic leaders also experience some real and unique forms of spiritual warfare. We've often said that if you want to avoid true and consistent spiritual body blows, simply show up at church to preach to the choir. Satan barely opens his drowsy eyes for that. But go to struggling communities where he's got everything bound up in chains and start setting people, places, and property free, and you've got a real fight. What we've found in kingdom work is that the attacks always correlate with the things you're trying to build. If you're building deep community, he attacks your friends with insecurity. If you are trying to build a financial infrastructure of generosity, wait for your refrigerator and your washing machine to quit working the same week your child breaks an arm and costs you $18,000. If you are trying to build a good reputation, wait for someone in your inner circle to lose their mind for a few hours and slander your name to some locals who are happy to spread the lie. If you are asking people to live at a level of covenantal commitment to share all things, wait for relational fights within the inner circle. Satan attacks what you are trying to build, so be aware and know it's coming. Teach, train, and model humility, open communication, forgiveness, a sense of humor, and more humility, and you'll make it through.

The Cost of Holding the Purse Strings

Can you imagine being entrusted with the little bag that held all of Jesus and his disciples' money? It probably wasn't a lot, but the pressure for Judas must have been great. In a real sense, these were the first missionary funds that were used to start the Jesus movement. But for Judas, having money didn't lead to success in the mission. In Alton, about two million dollars has come into our common purse through strange connections and charitable gifts—all through Hugh. And although he and his wife, Cheryl, are perceived to be the "owners" of Post Commons, they legally own nothing. Hugh is the president of the nonprofit organization that runs the enterprise, but because of the financial needs of starting a handful of businesses, as well as the challenges of COVID-19, and other factors, he takes no salary from inside the movement. He still has to get on planes to sing for his supper with speaking gigs, he's still taking house-painting jobs and other side hustles to help pay the bills (more about this a bit later), and he never really knows what is coming in on a month-by-month basis.

There's nothing wrong with pioneers financially profiting from the work in a business, nor is it strange that these types of leaders also garner personal supporters or patrons who help underwrite part of their financial needs, but apostolic leaders always face the pressure of minimizing their personal financial needs so that more money can be used for building the ecosystem. Thus, the pioneers play a general fundraising and fund-building role and have to prioritize the success of the businesses over their personal needs. They function like conduits, and—like a good businessperson—try to reinvest as much of the resources as possible back into the ecosystem.

Like Paul and other apostolic leaders, all those who raise funds must be very careful not to put themselves in a position where the funds "enure" to their benefit—a legal phrase specifying that the "officers" of a nonprofit cannot receive unfair benefits from the income or gifts given under their leadership. The truth is that the founding apostolic ones are usually responsible for nearly all the financial decisions, making it a constant challenge to manage resources wisely while also resisting the temptation to prioritize their donors' gain or their own personal financial gain over the mission.

The Cost of Getting Your Eye Right

It's telling that Jesus sandwiched his teaching about the eye being the lamp to the body between two well-known thoughts about mammon (Matthew 6:19–24). The first one says don't store up for yourself treasure on earth, and the second says you cannot serve both God and money. He knew that if our eyes are clear—meaning free from the love of money, free from the endless, dog-eat-dog pursuit of earthy treasures—the rest of the body will follow.

Every kingdom ecosystem has unique assets, opportunities, and access that make funding either easier or harder. Some have financial backers who help with the front-end capital, and some don't. Some get blessed with access to free spaces, and some don't. There's just no way to compare one to another, and you have to make sure you don't. If you do, your eyes will get blurry. Jesus taught that if our eyes are not right, our hearts will not be either (Luke 11:34). Often people come to Post Commons, the farm, the soccer field, or our central house, and you can read in their eyes the struggle they might be having with what they see. Some have even admitted that it caused them to judge us as people who got lucky or got the upper hand. Covetousness is real, but apostolic leaders will be the first to tell you that what you see isn't the whole story. The truth is that every great space or asset takes an incredible amount of work, sacrifice, and more sacrifice, and rarely do apostolic leaders have any unique benefit from what is established. Often they have to pay—both in time and money—to make it happen. So, we must guard our hearts and not look around at what others have. Let God create your story in whatever fashion he wants. If you're faithful with small things, he'll entrust you with larger things, and those larger things will take even more of your time, commitment, and money.

When you put these four systemic costs together, you find you must live, create, innovate, share, hold together, model, and release everything you do for the greater good ... all while being misjudged and maligned by those you serve and who watch from a distance. How's that for encouraging news?

We wanted to give you a heads-up before charting a course for that new community ecosystem you've dreamed of. If you are gifted apostolically, you've been called to suffer first, suffer often, and to receive judgments and critiques others won't get. Know your suffering will continue until the Lord puts an end to it. And if you're not apostolic, remember to support and resource these men and women who will lead the church in the future.

APOSTOLIC FUNDING

Every apostolic leader we've ever known is familiar with the pain of sharing their God-given vision with potential donors, only to come away feeling like they couldn't sell the vision or help the potential donor see what they see. Often, financial partners base their funding decisions on knowing all the outcomes and "betting on a sure thing." This approach could come from a denominational executive holding on to old or irrelevant metrics of scalability or from a private donor who made their wealth from being disciplined and conservative and whose financial strategy is to only invest in something that has a clear plan and almost cannot fail.

These "success metrics" might be valid when your only concern is the bottom line of financial growth, but the kingdom doesn't work on those principles alone. The most fundamental aspect of missions, as Hebrews 11 explains, is that a man or woman, especially an apostolic man or woman, is usually called to go out "on faith." Think about this dilemma. An apostolic leader hears the crazy call of God to go into an impoverished area to reveal God's kingdom, but then they have to prove to potential funders that they've got a solid plan that will be financially sustainable in three years.

The two really don't mesh. When Hugh's family went to Alton from Denver, all they knew was that God gave them a vision to do "something to help the town," as Hugh described it. Taylor, with two little kids and one on the way, also only knew he was to leave his church-pastor position, go from a good salary to nothing, and live among the poor. In either case, neither of us knew that coffee, a café, an events space, coworking, incubation, and thirty other unique aspects of brave cities would emerge.

Many donors also make apostolic leaders commit to old metrics or biased conditions. We know too many young, apostolically oriented leaders who still need to answer to denominations that don't let women teach or preach, and require a seminary degree and two years of "pastoral" experience before they'll be considered for church planting. Within six months, they'll be asked if they've had a worship gathering, or they'll be expected to apply the old metrics of numbers of "salvations" or baptisms as the yardstick for "wins" in the first year of work. Others have to hide every time they have a beer because, if they were seen drinking even once, they would be fired from their network.

How many times have we gotten funding and then lost it because our benefactors found out we weren't Trump supporters, Bernie supporters, Democrats, or Republicans? If we're on the wrong side of any political or social view, or put up a Facebook post they don't like, we kiss their money, prayers, and support goodbye.

Early on in our second church plant, a denomination offered me (Hugh) an insane amount of money to bring the story of our church plant under their brand. We were broke at the time, and it would have given us about a year of safe income … so it was tempting. The strings? Oh, only one. I couldn't consume alcohol. "So, you're saying I can have this income, and all I have to do is not have a beer with my neighbor when he asks?" "Yep," said the denominational leader, thinking he had me over the Jameson barrel. My final response was, "Well, my wife is going to think this is the most expensive drink I've ever had, but I'm going to have to say no to your one string. Having a glass of wine or beer with a neighbor is about as important a missionary activity as I know of, and I've been praying God would give me hundreds of these opportunities, so I can't agree to your conditions."

New wine and new wineskins need new winemakers, and winemakers need backing. Thus, the new winemakers are going to need people who love wine and trust the new leader to make it … or not. To settle for anything less will put you in a compromised position somewhere along the way. In other words, you'll lose your freedom to follow God.

So what's the answer? Well, you can take the money and worry about it later, which we don't recommend. Or you can say what you think the donor wants to hear, which we don't think stands up to the moral test of faith. Or you can just tell them you don't need their money and act like you can pull off the vision without funds. That doesn't work either, because all apostolic work needs funds, and the apostolic leader is rarely self-sustaining, at least at first. Apostolic types of the first order—the most gifted, the most proven—need capital partners and thus must always humbly see themselves as interdependent upon the body working as it should in partnership. But they should never partner with old metrics, old thinking, or old money.

To help you move toward better funding, consider the following options. But remember what the apostle Paul said in Romans 13:8, "Owe nothing to anyone—except for your obligation to love one another" (NLT). In other words, the freer you are from any other form of debt or strings, the easier it is to simply do the thing you are called to do. Also, in 1 Thessalonians 4:11, Paul tells us to make it our ambition to live a quiet life and work with our hands, so that we may not be dependent upon anybody.

So where's the balance? We do need help, and we must humbly

accept the interdependence with others that God is calling us to, so there's never any real sense that we are self-sufficient. But we cannot lose or compromise the vision given by God and make it palatable to those who can't see it. Nor should we ever feel pressure to meet others' expectations in order to accept their gifts. So, the best support comes from patrons, self-sustaining work, and multiple hats and buckets.

Patrons Over Donors

We believe there's a big difference between kingdom patrons and your average run-of-the-mill donor. Unlike the Medici family we talked about earlier, who funded Renaissance artists, normal donors typically look at traditional metrics, need to know their investment is yielding the return they want, and often have strings attached to their funds. For years, Lindsey and I (Taylor) were college and campus ministry leaders in one form or another. And for years we watched twenty-two-year-old aspiring campus ministers sent out to build a donor base. Although these ministers had very little experience or evidence of ministry faithfulness they could point to, and although they were full of anxiety about reaching their full funding, they had to sell themselves and their vision to the highest bidder. And then once they secured sufficient monthly recurring donations, they had to do everything they could to keep them coming, knowing that every year several donors would drop off for various reasons. To make matters worse, these men and women weren't blessed with huge networks to pull from and often found themselves feeling "less than" because of a lack of dollar signs in the win column.

That's why it is so vital to look for kingdom patrons—men and women God purposely links with apostolic leaders. God always seems to orchestrate a unique pathway to connect them, and that connection often seems to be lifelong. That's not to say there is always money flowing; there are more ways to stand with a pioneer than supporting them financially.

You cannot know the future, so when you are talking with potential kingdom partners, you shouldn't make grandiose promises. You should, however, have a responsible plan and be able to present some hoped-for kingdom markers. Apostolic types of leaders need apostolic types of investors who know that dead things need to come to life, ministry should be given freely, working with the poor doesn't scale or monetize, and restoration of boarded-up buildings and broken lives doesn't bring much of a tangible return. That is what the kingdom is about, so you're going to need some way to be able to stay true, stay strong, and stay pure if the foundation of an ecosystem is to endure.

It is helpful to have "patrons" who are giving to you personally, trusting you to establish, create, fix, tack to the left, tack to the right, scrap and start over, and make needed adjustments to the mission plan—men and women who will literally invest in the work they see God is doing and will do in you as a leader. For sure, these are hard to find; but, the last thing you want is to work hard for three to five years and then have someone pull funding because you had a beer with a neighbor, shared your support of some political figure, or marched in advocacy for police reform.

We're encouraged to see that many patrons with substantial wealth, or at least who give generously and sacrificially, are not just funding others; many are becoming artists themselves. They are people who have watched others "surf," and now they too are "surfing"; they've put their own wealth into new kingdom ventures that they themselves are now participating in. We also see patrons finding other patrons and working together toward significant city-building works where they combine resources and skills to affect larger issues.

Self-Sustaining Work

Most entrepreneurial ventures— business startups, real estate development, and most social justice works—require money up-front.

(You may need a little personal funding, too; more on that in the next section.) The goal is that you'll have enough resources to succeed; to not just limp by but eventually build out an economy that allows you to keep investing in your city and reach sustainability.

A good historical example of a business that supported community resources is The Dawn Settlement we referenced in act one. This abolitionist society of more than five hundred people sustained its community services through farmland, a sawmill, a gristmill, a brickyard, a rope manufacturing business, and a school.[5] Some brave cities we know are building revenue streams through coffee shops, t-shirt branding, hot chicken shacks, and the creation of handcrafted root beer. It really doesn't matter what you do, as long as it fits the context of the mission you are in. It may take you a while to get there, but keep working on enterprises that bless your city so that God can keep bringing his resources to you.

Multiple Hats ... Multiple Buckets

If you're going to live like a missionary on the front and fragile edge of a new work, you'll probably need a unique form of *personal* funding—and possibly many types of funding. We think Paul was teaching us a valuable lesson when he talked about tentmaking (Acts 18:3–4; 20:33–35). Tents are a metaphor for the kind of side hustle many of us engage in. And the same gifts and skills God has given us to pioneer brave cities are the ones we use to tent-make.

Hugh has multiple streams of income: donor funds, publishing royalties, coaching/consulting fees, speaking honorariums, house painting, Airbnb rental of their home, Cheryl's real estate business, fix-and-flip house profits, and whatever else comes along. Because of these funding streams, he doesn't take any salary from within the ecosystem or any of its businesses. Thus, being the president of the nonprofit, serving with brave cities, having a general "overseer" type pastoral role within the community, and maintaining an eighty-acre farm for his wife's equine therapy ministry are all volunteer efforts.

Taylor has quite a few startups under his belt, most of which he's given away, but he continues to receive income from them. The McCalls also live off donor funds, rental house revenues, house flips, property management income, Airbnb revenues, RV rental revenue, speaking and coaching revenue, and the income Lindsey earns from running a small financial firm they started. Thus, they serve as spiritual mothers and fathers in our community as volunteers.

Joe, a leader in Southern California, is one of the few apostolic leaders we've met along the way who has a single donor who covers 100 percent of their annual budget so they can simply do what they do. Yes, it makes us a bit jealous when we meet these types of fortunate leaders, but it's actually a great way to go if you can find your patron.

Stephanie, a Midwest leader, has pioneered an ecosystem from the ground up. She does take a salary from some of the businesses she created, but this is partly because of the amount of work and time she personally has put into them. She is always looking for ways to develop revenue streams to fund the work and free her up to create and innovate more while taking less from some of the initial businesses.

Hopefully, this gives you a better picture of how to keep your apostolic orientation out of the red! Your life will be about multiple roles, functions, and giftings so you'll most likely need multiple forms of funding.

APOSTOLIC PRIORITIES

When Paul said, "Follow my example as I follow the example of Christ" (1 Corinthians 11:1), he was telling us how apostolic leaders create movement from their lives, not their ministries. Paul, Jesus, and those who followed, couldn't call people to the gospel unless it was also good news for them personally.

During my (Hugh) third year of our first church plant in

Portland, Oregon, I reached a point of exhaustion. Because of my son's constant seizures, I had to take on a second job, while still painting houses and taking some seminary courses. Although it was difficult, I viewed 5 a.m. to 2 p.m. as my working hours and then used the afternoon and evenings to do the work of planting. I was tired and stressed ... but I thought that was just what you do.

One evening Cheryl called me into the kitchen and asked if we could have a chat. Somehow, I knew I was in trouble, and I was right. She started the conversation like this, "First, I want you to know that I love you, and I'm never going to leave you." *Uh-oh*, I thought. And then she continued, "But if you keep working this hard, giving all your relational energy to everyone who asks, and then jam in working twenty-five hours on your sermon prep from Thursday night to Sunday morning and don't leave any time for me or the kids, I don't think I'll ever enjoy living with you even one day." To top off this conversation, she invited my five-year-old daughter in and said, "Alli, tell Daddy what you said about him today." Alli looked right at me and said, "Daddy sucks."

With that little wake-up call, I asked a seasoned coach to help me rethink my life.

The first thing he suggested was that I own my life and calling. He said it this way, "God has gifted and called you to a unique life, but you have to live it. You can't let the world's pace, people's expectations, or the demands of building a church strip your life and marriage of the gospel. It's either good news for your entire family or it's the gospel of shitty news for everyone." Then he asked me to take two hours every Sunday night to plan out my next seven days.

As we got started, he helped me to see that my gifting angled toward the apostolic, entrepreneurial end of the ministry spectrum. I hadn't ever really heard that before, so it took me a while to get used to planning my schedule around these disciplines instead of the normal pastor and shepherd rhythms I felt every pastor just had to do. As I started to focus my energy on apostolic efforts, my personal life came into alignment; my stress went down, and the fruit went up.

As we grow in apostolic understanding, we find that things don't move in a straight line. The to-do list adjusts every day—sometimes every hour—and you have to learn to manage the integration of work, family, and spiritual momentum, both in discipling believers and wooing unbelievers. Forging and forming a decentralized network of leaders, communities, initiatives, and enterprises means no single day is ever the same, and the spiritual momentum happens along the way as opposed to in scheduled classes or timelines. Planning the week ahead is therefore about ensuring that you are making room for God to move as you juggle and hustle through many linked experiences.

A Day in the Life of an Apostle

So what's a typical day in my (Hugh's) life? I get asked this all the time. Initially, I thought about describing a normal day in half-hour increments; but as mentioned above, every day is very different and there are unique seasons when my focus is all in one area. As I've said, when we received a free building in Alton, I spent every day for about a year working mostly by myself renovating the space. Once it was done, my time moved to team recruitment and development as our coffee house and events businesses began to build out. During this time, we started working on the spiritual and communal focus that began to emerge. For most of the first three years after the café opened, I was in the "shop" every day, bussing tables, connecting with customers, and doing the things that would be considered "running the business." Now, five years in, I don't need to do anything related to the business. We have four gifted managers and a finance person who handle all the day-to-day administration. Thus, my next five years will be more focused on growing the network and the people in it, as I have more free time to be present as a "godfather." I also now have time to help other apostolic leaders around the globe. It's a natural progression of building a playing field others get to play on—I no longer need to quarterback it the whole time.

Nowadays, I may be painting a house for half a day and then meeting with our team the second half of the day. If I'm in a season where I'm not relying on physical labor for money but instead have apostolically raised funds or am living off other revenues, then it might look like this.

- 6 a.m.: Play golf with guys in our community and one nonbelieving guy we've been inviting into our community.
- 10 a.m.: Go to Post Commons to connect with our team, barista staff, and locals who are passing through.
- 11 a.m.: Meet with our coffee manager and finance manager talking logistics and admin stuff and ordering booze for an event.
- Noon: Do a CrossFit workout—sweating but connecting with four folks who are in our missional community who are not yet believers.
- 2 p.m.: Have coffee with Cheryl, and time with grandkids around the pool.
- 4 p.m.: Lead a training webinar for an Australian church-planting network ($500).
- 5 p.m.: Have dinner.
- 7 p.m.: Spend strategic time with some of our missionary team members.

As you can see, every day is a combination of leadership time, evangelistic time, family time, and a little admin time—and, along the way, I get in a workout for needed personal time.

On the weekends, I am usually working an event at Post Commons and enjoying a Sunday sabbath experience with our missionary community. Sometimes that is a simple two-hour gathering, and sometimes it's an all-day time around the pool with some fun and some spiritual focus together.

Taylor's schedule is just as varied. He longs to see churches in every city and every country functioning as kingdom ecosystems, so half the time he's working with leaders all over the world. As an apostolic team, Taylor and Lindsey's priority is being great neighbors, blessing their block and the people around them in whatever ways they can. Locally, they float to wherever the most pressing need exists. Taylor loves to start new things and empower leaders to live out their dreams. If a new team member joins us with a vision of starting a wood shop mentoring business, Taylor may spend twelve months helping him build out the shop. Or he may be driving all over St. Louis to basketball tournaments with the first-ever Alton AAU basketball team we started. On spare evenings, they focus their mentoring time with our key leaders from 8 p.m. to 11 p.m., after all their kids are down. That's while raising five kids and running multiple side hustles to pay the bills.

Apostolicing is about constantly activating environments and experiences that foster momentum with leaders and lost people. As we've said, apostolic leaders are creating kingdom ecosystems that will serve as the bones for a larger network of ministry and business instead of focusing just on one localized congregational point. A key change from a pastoral to an apostolic orientation is that pastors often give time to anyone, whereas apostolic leaders must strategically limit their time almost exclusively to leaders or lost people.

Most leaders we coach have gotten used to spending most of their time with folks who are *not* leaders (people taking responsibility for other people) and *not* lost people. Another way to say this is that most leaders spend their time with the "multitude"—people who don't intend to lead or sacrifice, nor people who need to find Jesus. This may not be bad, but it isn't strategic.

Jesus loved the multitude and even wept as he watched them, but he never gave his strategic time to them. He had just three years to change the course of history, so he spent the majority of his time discipling leaders who would carry a lot of weight, or with people who would be transformed by the gospel. Both of these groups create the momentum almost every leader hopes to see.

So as you plan for apostolic fruit, commit to giving your best time to work, family, leaders, and the lost. If you stay in those four zones, you'll get momentum. If you don't spend your time in these four zones, you'll get exhausted and discouraged for lack of fruit.

Finally, you may be asking how an apostolic leader connects with and is able to retreat and hear from God. And this answer is as creative and varied as the funding options we've explored. Some still hold to daily patterns of devotional time, some make a weekly sabbath a true sabbath, and some are more aesthetic and connect with God through the actual work itself. We've mentioned several times that, for the Benedictines, prayer really was the work and the work really was prayer, and they expected to hear from God in activity as much as in solitude. Most apostolic leaders have personal spiritual rhythms, team spiritual rhythms, and family spiritual rhythms. Apostolic leaders are also spiritually encouraged by spending time with other apostolic leaders. But for sure, our walk with God is based on walking with him both devotionally and intentionally into mission as an integrated way of life instead of disintegrated compartments of life.

EPILOGUE

Coming Out of Babylonian Ways

After this I saw another angel coming down from heaven. He had great authority, and the earth was illuminated by his splendor. With a mighty voice he shouted:
"'Fallen! Fallen is Babylon the Great!'
She has become a dwelling for demons
and a haunt for every impure spirit,
a haunt for every unclean bird,
a haunt for every unclean and detestable animal.
For all the nations have drunk
the maddening wine of her adulteries.
The kings of the earth committed adultery with her,
and the merchants of the earth grew rich from her excessive luxuries."
Then I heard another voice from heaven say:
"'Come out of her, my people,'
so that you will not share in her sins."
REVELATION 18:1–4

We started with a surfing analogy, so we want to end there as well. My (Hugh's) buddy Mark not only taught me about the surfing community and its life, but he also invited me to surf with his people. Like I said, it was scary, exhausting, beautiful, more dramatic than I had imagined, and more peaceful than I thought possible—but most of all, it caused me to ponder what type of life and faith I would live in a small town one thousand miles away from any ocean. Something about seeing Mark's culture, lived in community, turned some lightbulbs on for me in my hopes for my own community.

FYI, he didn't let me use a blue board. Instead, he lent me one of his custom-made boards—and made sure he was literally within five feet of me the entire time. I remember him showing me the wave patterns from the shore and talking me through how we would enter the water so we wouldn't get bashed against the rocks. Just as we were about to get in, he threw me for a loop by telling me that the waters we were about to surf also served as the largest great-white-shark mating area in the US. That part didn't help! When we got out there, he showed me how the "lineup" works and pointed out some blue-boarders who weren't respecting surfing etiquette. Then he simply said, "If you don't freak out and just do exactly what I tell you, you'll ride a wave today." I did exactly what he said … and I rode a wave. Mark gave me a glimpse of surfing not as a hobby, a sport, or a magazine picture. He wooed me into living the experience with him.

You may have picked up by now that I'm the old guy and Taylor is a younger man. I'm ahead of him by almost two decades, but I remember meeting him and Lindsey, listening to their story, and picking up the subtle frequencies of not only how they did life but also how they saw the story of God in Scripture. They spoke about verses I had studied and preached my whole life, but when Taylor talked, I always felt as if I was being invited to go deeper … and I loved the feeling, even as an old guy.

What we've experienced in our Alton brave city, and what we've seen and heard from other brave city communities around the US, makes us feel like we have found a secret passageway through all the old stuff to a new, integrated, and full-hearted way to follow Jesus. Each of the brave cities we know of has learned to "surf" and has developed truly inspiring communities. Sharing their stories brings them joy, and they often say, "I could never go back to the old way of church."

And this is what we hoped for you in writing this book. We want you to trade in your blue board and consider finding a community of people who care as much about the church as Mark's friends care about the integrity of surfing. Just as Jesus loved the multitudes, we love the "blue- boarders" of the church, and we hope many of them will grow weary of weekend, recreational faith. However, we didn't write this book to try to coerce or critique them. They have probably never seen an alternative option, so all they can go by is whether or not church in its present form is meaningful for them. Our guess is that, over time, it will prove not to be, and they may be open to a more integrated experience of life, faith, and church.

But for you—the archaeologists, artists, and architects—we hope we gave you some well-needed permission and encouragement to keep going in your alternative way of responding to Jesus' call on your life. Even if you are not understood and even if at times it seems like you are pushing water uphill, you will see fruit if you stick at it. You don't have to go back! You are free in every sense of the word because where Jesus is, there is freedom; and for freedom, Christ has set you free (see 2 Corinthians 3:17; Galatians 5:1). So, fail if you must, fight at all times, but for sure, don't go back to what felt like a strange religious bondage.

COME OUT OF BABYLON!

In Revelation 18, John shares the harsh reality of "Babylon"—a fallen place that simply will never deliver what the kingdom can. Babylon has become a metaphor for opposition to the rule of

God by world powers, or the exile of God's people from the land of blessing. Beyond that, it also symbolizes the wickedness of the world; we "come out of Babylon" when we refuse to partake of the sins of the world.[1] It is that invitation to "come out of her ... so that you will not share in her sins" that John records as originating from a voice from heaven in verse four.

And so, our final invitation is to come out of any form of religion that feels more like the Babylonian world with all of its controls, hang-ups, diversions, and pressures—to turn your back on the "normal way of life" that people settle for, which slowly dulls us, so we become asleep spiritually. We have high respect for any pastor of any type of church. It's a hard life, and the pressures and disappointments are real. Some of it is just part of loving people, but now we realize much of the miseries are self-imposed, and God never intended for you to put up with Babylonian drama. There's going to be a fight no matter what you choose to do, but maybe from here on out, you can fight the good fight instead of fighting for your soul.

This "coming out" of Babylon is not just meant for individuals; it's meant for movements, for communities, for churches. A city within a city is in the world but is not tethered to it. A brave city, instead, is like the catacombs—a refuge for people to find when all else has let them down. This is who and what the church was meant to be. Not a poor business model dependent on the next great speaker to bring in the crowds or the dough. Not a counseling center attempting to help people get through life. And not a gathering space that masquerades as a community epicenter. It was meant to be a city. A family. A movement. God's presence on earth. Brave cities inhabit neighborhoods, businesses, and all broken places. The call to come out of Babylon means for us to form a different city—a city that functions with a different set of principles—and to be a people who live and bless the areas we're in. Remember, "When the righteous prosper, the city rejoices" (Proverbs 11:10).

YOU'VE GOTTA SERVE SOMEBODY

Recent world events have hit like an earthquake, and the landscape has been permanently altered. COVID-19 may have stuck a fork in a lot of struggling churches, but dinner was over a long time ago. Instead of just returning to normal, the pandemic allowed the church to try something more substantial. However, most just reverted to what they knew as soon as they could. But nothing was the same. It will look to some like the church is decimated, and they will lament the destruction that is left behind; but we see the remains as rubble to rebuild that we and God can use together to build a new city.

The scripture in Revelation is a call to make a decision. And the decision is costly, but it is simple. It's about what city you want to serve. If you pick Babylon, you will have to serve it fully. You can try to serve both worlds, but Jesus repeatedly taught the principle of all-in, burn-the-bridge-behind-you discipleship. The great theologian Bob Dylan repeated Jesus' and Paul's words by singing you're going to serve somebody, either the devil or the Lord, but you're going to serve somebody.[2] Jesus said in Matthew 6:24, "No one can serve two masters. Either you will hate the one and love the other, or you will be devoted to the one and despise the other."

Jesus never, ever gave an option for being double-minded, double-tongued, or duplicitous in our affections. He always called for allegiance. He didn't do that to be a priggish, arrogant king, but because he knew his kingdom city was so much better for us than a zip code outside the kingdom of God. He knew the kingdom of Babylon would not allow you to be your true God-given self and that it would continuously trick you into thinking that it offers life for you and your family, but it doesn't. The ways of Babylon won't deliver. But the kingdom of God, lived and discovered in small intentional communities, will.

So come with us, out of Babylon, to deeper, scarier waters. Learn to live the full life by dying to self; then invite others to observe with fascination and to come and die, too. And let's see a new renaissance of kingdom artists architecting and digging up new treasure!

A REMINDER OF SOME THINGS WE'VE SAID

Here is a catalog of what we believe and are calling you to live out:

- The gospel isn't just Jesus. Jesus, his life, death, and resurrection AND the kingdom of God here on earth is the gospel. If we relegate the gospel to just Jesus, then we are thankful for what he did, and we will worship him; but if we understand the gospel as the continuing work of the kingdom on earth, then we must also follow Jesus and work with him.
- Our work is to believe what Jesus believes, demonstrating as we proclaim and proclaiming as we demonstrate that the powers of darkness are disarmed.
- Kingdom ecosystems are developed through integrated, interdependent covenant communities, and are made up of active disciples who link benevolent businesses, justice works, and intentional neighborhood homes.
- Business isn't for mission, or a means to fund mission, but instead business *is* mission.
- "Hybrid" approaches don't work. Missionaries and consumers don't coexist well. New wine must be put in new wineskins, while the old wineskins are honored but not forced to change. Consumerism must *not* be an option in a brave city because it co-opts the kingdom ecosystem.
- Money must be dislodged from the mission except for business development and benevolent service to the kingdom ecosystem.
- All the functions and activities of the church should and can be done for no pay, thus freeing up all the church's resources to build kingdom ecosystems.

- Leadership for this emerging form of church needs to come from those who have the apostolic, evangelistic, and prophetic giftings given in Ephesians 4, and this must be supported by shepherds and teachers, so that the church will become mature. But the apostolic must lead.
- In this ecosystem, there is no ceiling based on gender, age, or profession. Everyone can serve in their gifting, in "due season," without the pressure of being everyone's pastor or leader.
- Most of the existing church measurements and metrics, and thus pressures, are things Jesus told us not to measure. His way is freer, more fun, and far more reproducible. Thus, we only carry the weight of faithfulness.
- A small covenant community of mission will bear far more fruit than a large recreational, consumer country club.
- We can't grow or build the kingdom, but we can plant and build things that God grows and builds his kingdom with.
- The church of Jesus must not become a fourth place isolated from the first, second, and third places of home, work, and play. When it does, it by nature becomes irrelevant—a stench instead of an aroma.
- There is only Jesus' way, and his way only works if we refuse to submit to the Babylonian way. We cannot live both ways.
- Marketplace mission, although hard, may be the only way to fund the next generation of church leaders, especially from minority and under-resourced communities. As the tithe and donor-charity models struggle, adding enterprise to our ventures has a much better chance of sustaining the work and the workers.
- Church as a city works best and has the most impact in underserved towns, cities, and regions, where proclamation must be linked with justice work.
- Disciple-making must be linked to shared business and mission enterprise instead of continuing the isolated, weekly Bible study.

- Church gatherings or worship services don't have to be public. A speakeasy form of gathering God's people together limits the leaven of the Pharisees and keeps the church as a family growing at a pace that keeps the covenant and DNA intact.

In our brave cities, let's imitate the great Creator, the Iconoclast Jesus, and his avant-garde community. Let's create. Let's make music instead of math. Let's uncover the kingdom like archaeologists, and architect only enough to hold the art we are creating. Let's make new wine in new wineskins and leave the leaven of the Pharisees behind in Babylon, where it belongs. Let's hang with the real bear in his natural habitat. Let's surf!

Tell us how it goes! Share your story, and find other brave-city inspiration, at bravecities.com.

Shalom,

Taylor and Hugh

SAMPLE GRAY PAPER

We wanted to give you a sample of what we're calling a "gray paper" on www.bravecities.com. White papers are the normal name for contextual learnings, but since nothing is black and white, we think it's better to call them gray papers.

We created www.bravecities.com to provide timely coaching and inspiration for those of you crazy enough to get out in front of this changing missional context, and the website will feature gray papers written by practitioners in our network. We hope you will soon be contributing a few gray papers with best practices, worst practices, and anything else you think will help the next ecosystem builder.

We think these gray papers may actually be more important than most of what we've said in the book. Enjoy!

A RETHINK ON CHURCH PLANTING
BY HUGH HALTER AND TAYLOR MCCALL

In Matthew 10, Jesus sends out the first twelve church planters. In Luke 10, Jesus sends out seventy-two. The approach in these accounts is so similar, it appears that Jesus might have had the same strategy with both groups. If that's the case, there may be some gold to mine in these texts. We'll focus on Matthew 10 and look at the sense of timing, the order of priority, and some critical missionary nuances. As with most stories, you can't just pick and choose what you like or understand and blow off what you don't. What we must look for is a contextual framework for how to build a kingdom ecosystem in a neighborhood, town, city, or region.

First, Jesus tells his disciples to take nothing with them. No bag, no purse, no sandals. This goes against every ounce of

174 | BRAVE CITIES

modern church-planting strategy, which is usually centered on the same concepts as choosing where to start a new Chick-fil-A. Historically, denominations only support a new work when it fits their metrics, such as general demographics, issues of competition, standard of living, or whether the target group will be able to tithe and support the new work. The planter, of course, has to go through a rigorous process to receive start-up support and often subsidizes any potential for failure with project fundraising and personal support.

But Jesus says his disciples need nothing. He's clearly not saying to live naked and have no possessions; he's saying he'll provide everything they need as they go, and to not wait to go because the fields are ripe for harvest. Sure, donors will come. Money will come. Support will come. But we don't need that in order to be sent. In fact, he seems to be saying, don't seek it.

In our experience, most people who carve out a legitimate ecosystem generally begin with very little except a vision and a few friends—if they're lucky. Yes, in Hugh's story in Alton, a building was donated as well as $650,000, but those were only provided after he and Cheryl went to Alton with nothing more than a sense of calling and no idea about any of this future provision. We suggest you risk placing your entire hope on Jesus alone building the ecosystem, instead of hedging a bet that you can pull it off because you're funded ... in case God doesn't show up. We believe this first instruction is about testing motives and the strength of our faith and dependency, as well as knowing that whatever does unfold will be much more likely to be from Jesus, thus settling the issue that only *he* should get the glory.

Second, Jesus mentions a person of peace or "favor" that rests upon us as we connect with people. Some try to interpret this exclusively as looking for an actual person—like "Bob was my 'person of peace.'" But while Bob may be an actual person of peace, it's important to think more broadly about the initial season of ministry, where we focus on getting the favor of the people who then peaceably connect us with others, who in turn also extend the peace and favor to us as a movement. In simple terms, in this first season (three to five years) you should be working for the spirit of favor that will rest on you, your team, and your work over time. This "person" or spirit of favor comes through presence, commitment, devotion, social blessing … in essence, making the city better. It's built practically through things like simply being present and known by your neighbors, being available, serving the needs in your community, being liked and enjoyed by people, and throwing block parties and cookouts in your neighborhood (without trying to convert people). It's gained through launching local businesses that bless the community, such as coffee shops, community centers, and gyms—any social space that brings people together and increases the unity and camaraderie in your town.

How do you know if you've found peace and favor? The town will tell you. We never toot our own horn, but we do tell one another if someone who doesn't follow Jesus speaks highly of someone else in our community or about a work we're involved with. Alton is half Black and half white, with all the normal issues related to that. In the downtown area, there's been only one Black-owned business—just one block away from Post Commons. Yvonne, the owner, was a light who loved Jesus but also loved her Black and brown community, and she loved to make pies. Everyone knew her, and she had a huge following. In July 2022, she was killed in a vehicle accident while on vacation, at the age of forty-four. Word quickly spread and $100,000 was raised within a few days to help support her children. The town was clearly in mourning.

We didn't think it was a big deal, but we offered to host an after-party following her public memorial service. People knew Hugh was close to Yvonne, but it demonstrated a great sense of favor that a Black family and the Black community wanted to be in a predominantly white-owned building. All we know is that trust, legitimate friendship, peace, and favor were flowing like a river that night, and we were humbled to know God had been at work as we all gathered downtown.

Many traditional church planters roll into a town, and within six months are inviting people to their church service, only to experience rejection. That's the opposite of what we're talking about. You *should* be rejected if you move that fast. If you try to get people to trust you spiritually before they give and receive peace and favor, you're getting what you deserve, and you cannot call that evidence that the people are hard-hearted. They're just smart, and you'll be the fool who moved too fast, based on the metrics of your denomination instead of on Matthew 10.

And of course, Jesus says, if no peace comes, then leave the town and shake the dust off your shoes. I would leave, too, if we had put in five hard years earning respect and favor but never got any. But we think if you put in the time, you won't ever have to shake off any dust.

Third, once peace is developed, Jesus says to heal the sick and cleanse the lepers. Some read this and are relieved that their town doesn't have any lepers left, but this instruction can be read as doing works of grace and justice among the poor, lonely, outcast, and broken in your city. This is the work of finding and blessing the untouchables in the community and doing practical work to see people's circumstances change.

As in James 5:13–15, think of leprosy as almost a sickness of poverty. The opposite of poverty is not wealth; it's worth. There are the men, women, and children who are weighed down by the cares of this world, by the systems of this world, by one bad decision after another. The lepers are the outcasts, the ones no one wants to touch or be near—the unclean. The healing comes in an open table, a family, and a purpose. The forgiveness of sin and the anointing of oil, like James says, are a result of this healing. Practical examples of this effort to bring healing include doing justice work in housing provision, education, job creation; providing fine dinners for the homeless; embracing single mothers and the fatherless; opening winter warming centers; and offering mentoring programs for youth.

Fourth, casting out demons. This last instruction in the progression is the one no one today wants to do, unless we understand what Jesus is saying. Demons, the demonic, and salvation go together. When demons are removed, people are free to follow and serve Jesus. This is where the power of Jesus invading the hearts and minds of others becomes real. This is about evangelism and even revival.

In Matthew 12, Jesus warns against an unclean spirit leaving a person without something filling the void. If the space is left empty, the spirit will come back with seven more spirits worse than the first. The space must be filled with the Spirit of God and the hope and good news of the kingdom. To make this possible, we begin to invite others into repentance, surrender, and devotion. This can manifest itself in deeper, more liturgical forms of worship, communion, prayer, and the full life of the community. We don't evangelize and then invite people to some discipleship class; we invite them to be adopted into the family on a mission where every part of their being will be renovated.

Here's a summary:

1. **Take Nothing With You**
   - Go in faith to the places you're called.
   - Don't worry about money or provision.

   Make holiness and prayerful discernment the priority of this time, so you can tune in to the voice of God.

2. **Look for Peace and Favor**
   - Show grace, bring peace, and build favor in your city.
   - Serving is key. Presence is key. Consistency is key.
   - Build contextual convergence spaces—coffee shops, pubs, gyms, community centers. Bring blessing and innovation to a city.

This prepares the way for the good news of the kingdom to be preached.

3. **Heal the Sick and Cleanse the Lepers**
   - Heal the sick, which can include both physical and spiritual sickness.
   - Welcome those who are outcast, lonely, and poor.
   - Turn your eyes to the margins. Get out of your comfort zone. Have a strong prophetic ethic against showing partiality to the rich and influential.

   Here, we create options, start businesses with easy entry, and raise money for the marginalized, not just our own thing.

4. **Cast Out Demons**
   - Invite people into the salvation and liberty that comes with knowing and following Jesus. The invitation is to our decentralized missional communities, homes, and smaller disciple-making communities, as well as larger family gatherings, training, and worship experiences.
   - Baptize—embody freedom from bondage.
   - Pray for true revival.

   Here, captives are set free, worship ensues, and God's glory is made known in our context.

NOTES

Prologue: The Day Everything Changed in Surfing and the Church

1. Paul Walker, "The American Church Has Lost One Million People Since COVID Lockdowns," July 30, Medium (reprinted from Backyard Church), https://medium.com/backyard-theology/the-american-church-has-lost-one-million-people-since-covid-lockdowns-269b05838997.

2. *Gidget*, directed by Paul Wendkos (1959; Culver City, CA: Columbia Pictures).

3. Jake Meador, "The Misunderstood Reason Millions of Americans Stopped Going to Church," *The Atlantic*, July 29, 2023, https://www.theatlantic.com/ideas/archive/2023/07/christian-church-communitiy-participation-drop/674843/.

Act One: Music Not Math

1. We'll say more about this in act four.

2. "Word: Why is jazz not part of the pop scene anymore?" *Undernews*, August 30, 2021, https://prorevnews.blogspot.com/2021/08/word-why-is-jazz-not-part-of-pop-scene.html.

3. *Rob Roy*, directed by Michael Caton Jordan (1995; Los Angeles, CA: United Artists).

4. *Anthony Bourdain: No Reservations*, season 2, episode 13, "Special: Decoding Ferran Adrià," aired July 3, 2006, Travel Channel, https://www.imdb.com/title/tt0944989/.

5. Harriet Beecher Stowe, *Uncle Tom's Cabin* (1852; repr., New York: Vintage Books, 1991).

6. Wayne Kelly, "Inside Uncle Tom's Cabin," *Heritage Matters*, February 12, 2005, https://www.heritage-matters.ca/articles/inside-uncle-toms-cabin.

Act Two: Archaeology, Artistry, and Architecture

1. C. S. Lewis, *The Lion, the Witch and the Wardrobe* (New York: HarperCollins, 1950), 75.

2. "Michelangelo Quotes," BrainyQuote.com, BrainyMedia Inc, 2023, accessed November 2, 2023, https://www.brainyquote.com/quotes/michelangelo_386296.

3. "Supernatural Seminar with Dr. Michael Heiser | Part Four," YouTube, https://youtu.be/1ZzCHKfx6Os (see around minutes 23–26).

4. Walter Wink, *Jesus and Nonviolence: A Third Way* (Minneapolis, MN: Augsburg Fortress Press, 2003).

5. *1883*, mini-series directed by Taylor Sheridan (December 19, 2021; Paramount+).

Act Three: Kingdom Ecosystems

1   Staff Reporter, "Stop Soil Erosion," Ecologist, January 9, 2020, https://theecologist.
    org/2020/jan/09/stop-soil-erosion.
2   Brit Holewinski, "Underground Networking: The Amazing Connections Beneath
    Your Feet," National Forest Foundation, accessed November 8, 2023, https://www.
    nationalforests.org/blog/underground-mycorrhizal-network.

Act Four: Free Market Church

1   Staff, "Atheists More Motivated by Compassion than the Faithful," LiveScience, May
    01, 2012, https://www.livescience.com/20005-atheists-motivated-compassion.
    html.
2   Jonathan Cornford, "The Manna Economy," Manna Gum, August 2017, https://
    www.mannagum.org.au/manna_matters/august-2017/bible_and_economy.
3   Ched Myers, "Jesus' New Economy of Grace," Sojourners, July-August 1998, https://
    sojo.net/magazine/july-august-1998/jesus-new-economy-grace.
4   Kevin Breuninger, "Trump brags about Dow 30,000 at surprise news conference,
    leaves after a minute," CNBC, November 24, 2020, https://www.cnbc.com/
    amp/2020/11/24/trump-brags-about-dow-30000-at-surprise-press-conference-
    leaves-after-a-minute.html.
5   Milton Friedman, "A Friedman doctrine—The Social Responsibility of Business Is
    to Increase Its Profits," The New York Times Magazine, September 13, 1970, https://
    www.nytimes.com/1970/09/13/archives/a-friedman-doctrine-the-social-respon-
    sibility-of-business-is-to.html.
6   "BlackRock, Inc.: Implementation plan for new Business Roundtable 'Purpose
    of a Corporation,'" As You Sow, December 10, 2020, https://www.asyousow.org/
    resolutions/2020/12/10/blackrock-inc-implementation-plan-for-new-business-
    roundtable-purpose-of-a-corporation.
7   Barbara Novick, "A Fundamental Reshaping of Finance," Harvard Law School
    Forum on Corporate Governance, January 16, 2020, https://corpgov.law.harvard.
    edu/2020/01/16/a-fundamental-reshaping-of-finance/.
8   "Trappist beer," Wikipedia, https://en.wikipedia.org/wiki/Trappist_beer.
9   Ian Paul, "What was slavery like in the NT world?" Psephizo, September 20, 2019,
    https://www.psephizo.com/biblical-studies/what-was-slavery-like-in-the-nt-world/.
10 "Capitalism," Wikipedia, https://en.wikipedia.org/wiki/Capitalism; "Free market,"
    Wikipedia, https://en.wikipedia.org/wiki/Free_market.
11 "In the Old Testament, the Hebrew word shalom is usually translated 'peace' and
    refers to Israel's hope for all things to be set right again. It can include a personal
    sense of wellbeing, but it also has social and political dimensions. Shalom involves
    being right with God and with past enemies. It means community, justice, and the
    end of all divisions and hatreds. True shalom includes peace with God, with others,

with the world, and even with the earth itself." Michael Frost, *Mission Is the Shape of Water: Learning From the Past to Inform Our Role in the World Today* (Cody, WY: 100 Movements Publishing, 2023), 23–24.

Act Five: Orders of Desire

1. *Forrest Gump,* directed by Robert Zemekis (1994; Culver City, CA: The Tisch Company).
2. Kristin Arzt, "Guide To Sword Making: Learn How To Forge A Sword," Guides To Industrial Art, accessed November 17, 2023, https://www.thecrucible.org/guides/bladesmithing/sword-making/.
3. Though not all scholars agree, church discipline is portrayed as a necessary element of a "true" church. See Michael Matossian, "Word, Sacrament, and Discipline: Discipline, a True Mark?" *Place for Truth*, December 21, 2018, https://www.place-fortruth.org/blog/word-sacrament-and-discipline-discipline-true-mark.

Act Six: Kingdom Ecclesiology

1. Lance Ford, *UnLeader: Reimagining Leadership ... and Why We Must* (Kansas City: Beacon Hill Press, 2012), 94.
2. "The Cell and the Coracle," *The Cell and the Coracle*, accessed November 22, 2023, https://thecellandcoracle.wordpress.com/about/.
3. Phil Carradice, "The Celts," waleshistory, January 7, 2011, https://www.bbc.co.uk/blogs/waleshistory/2011/01/the_celts.html.
4. Lynne Baab, "Celtic Christianity: Community," *Lynne Baab*, May 15, 2015, https://www.lynnebaab.com/blog/friendship-loneliness-and-prayer-praying-2.
5. "Speakeasy," Wikipedia, https://en.wikipedia.org/wiki/Speakeasy.
6. *Merriam-Webster.com*, 2023, s.v. "sacrament," https://www.merriam-webster.comdictionary/sacrament.
7. "About Us," Idle Roasting Co., https://www.idleroasting.com/about.
8. See "Fastest-Growing Churches in America," *Outreach 100*, 2023, https://outreach100.com/fastest-growing-churches-in-america.

Act Seven: Apostolicing

1. "Apostle–Apostolos (Greek Word Study)," Precept Austin, July 25, 2017, https://www.preceptaustin.org/apostle_-_apostolos.
2. Alan Hirsch, *5Q: Reactivating the Original Intelligence and Capacity of the Body of Christ* (Atlanta, GA: 100 Movements, 2017); Neil Cole, *Primal Fire: Reigniting the Church with the Five Gifts of Jesus* (Carol Stream, IL: Tyndale House Publishers, 2009).
3. See "Shalia," Wikipedia, https://en.wikipedia.org/wiki/Shaliah.
4. "Don't Miss Out," FTX Super Bowl ad, 2022, https://www.youtube.com/watch?v=_-FQqo46CJQ.

[5] "Black settlement in Ontario," Ontario Heritage Trust, accessed December 13, 2023, https://www.heritagetrust.on.ca/pages/our-stories/slavery-to-freedom/history/black-settlement-in-ontario.

Epilogue: Coming Out of Babylonian Ways

[1] Ron J. Bigalke Jr., "Babylon as Metaphor," Wiley Online Library, November 25, 2011, https://onlinelibrary.wiley.com/doi/10.1002/9780470670606.wbecc0108.

[2] See Bob Dylan, "Gotta Serve Somebody," 1979, track #1 on *Slow Train Coming*, Columbia Records.

ABOUT THE AUTHORS

TAYLOR MCCALL has been a serial entrepreneur from a young age and began serving in traditional ministry in 1999. For the past fifteen years, he and his wife, Lindsey, have been working in urban communities and planting churches, and have started or helped start over twenty businesses, as well as a business incubator that's launched many more. Along with their five kids, they live in Alton, Illinois, working with Hugh Halter and the Lantern Network.

Taylor believes the church was always meant to look like an integrated ecosystem functioning as a city within a city. He and Lindsey coach and consult leaders all over the world to see intentional community, marketplace endeavors, and kingdom justice works function and flow within the movement of the local body. Together with Hugh, Taylor is crafting the Brave Cities movement that offers insight and invitation into this way of life and church.

HUGH HALTER has been a leading voice and missional guide for over thirty years. He has authored books such as *The Tangible Kingdom, AND, Flesh, BIVO,* and *Righteous Brood.*

Hugh speaks extensively across the globe, encouraging innovative forms of church, and when home loves to help his wife, Cheryl, run Rí Beag Refuge, an equine therapy farm. He co-directs Brave Cities and is the founder of Lantern Network in Alton, Illinois.

You can find Hugh and various resources at hughhalter.com or bravecities.com.

Made in the USA
Columbia, SC
15 October 2024

44415337R00111